FIGHTING FOR
LIFE AND JUSTICE

FIGHTING FOR LIFE AND JUSTICE

*Being the First Just Say No Kid
& Baby of the Gangsters/Mobsters.
How to Fight Law, Judicial Corruption.*

R. Wunderlich

Word Art Publishing
9350 Wilshire Blvd
Suite 203, Beverly Hills, CA 90212
www.wordartpublishing.com
Phone: 1 (888) 614 - 1370

Published by Word Art Publishing

ISBN: Paperback   978-1-955070-17-1
          Ebook   978-1-955070-18-8

Dedication to my mother she's my teacher,

best friend and my mother

Thank you God for my mother and father.

Thank you God for showing me mercy and love...

Thanks also my Friend R.A...

"Some Names and Places have been changed to protect the true identity. Everything in the book is correct and true. Also I would like to add Not all law enforcement and judges are bad. But unfortunately the bad one's make the job's harder for the good one's. My mother was going to boot out the bad one's by running for sheriff and the 1st thing she was going to do is a TRUE CITIZENS REVIEW BOARD, With the powers to suspend, fire and when charges were found to be true against the officer they would turn evidence over to the district attorney's office to prosecute. She wanted to restore respect to the office of law enforcement by reviving PROTECT AND SERVE. We need to return the powers to the citizens. We The People."

I AM R. WUNDERLICH. This is my story of my life.

I was born somewhere in California on July of 1969 to the parents of B. Wunderlich. and G. Wunderlich.

My dad was a flower grower somewhere in California. He grew flowers to be shipped all over the world. He sold his property and went to work for flower growers and shippers. He worked there until he passed away on December 24, 1980.

He was in and out of the hospital for four years. He had leukemia, a disease of the blood cells. Mom and I would go visit with him every night after she got off work. He was a wonderful dad and husband. Before he got sick, he took me everywhere he went. By the way, my dad was the baby of the Gangsters and Mobsters of California. They were known as the Wunderlich and Famous Gangster family in California. They were so well known that he was in the book "Gangsters of California" by the author. The book came out in 2013. The movie followed. I will have a few more tidbits about my dad throughout my story.

My mother was born and raised somewhere in Florida. She later moved to somewhere in Florida where she joined the police department. After two years she went to Ocala, Florida to college. She studied law. Her mother became very sick and she had to quit school and go back to a place somewhere in Florida to take care of her. She worked at Borden's Dairy as a milk delivery person. As a milkmaid, she was sent by the company to somewhere up north to be a guest on the television show "What's My Line". She won the $500 prize because they could not guess her occupation.

She went to California on vacation and met my dad, and never went home. They made a great couple together. I am a product of their great marriage.

When I was born, I was the star of the entire family. They called me "Master". After all, I was the baby of the family. By the way, I forgot to say that my father was much older than my mother. Dad was already in his 50s and Mom was in her 30s.

I am the best thing that came out of their marriage. In 1979, mom was asked by the agent of advertising for a major toy company if she would let me do commercials for the company. So I became a Mattel baby. I did a lot of different toys until I was a year old, when my agent asked if I would do a new doll commercial. I could have had the role because I had long, blonde, curly hair. However, my dad said "No son of mine will be dressed up like a girl". He made sure of that. That same day he took me to a barber shop and had my hair cut off. That ended my commercial contract.

When I was two years old, I had a severe ear infection in my right ear. Mom kept taking me to Children's Hospital almost every day. They would give me a shot of antibiotic and send me home. This went on for almost three weeks. I went into convulsions. Mom sent my sister to get a nurse that lived in our building. Ethel, the nurse, came in and put me in a tub of cool water and rubbing alcohol until my fever went down. She told my mom that we should go to Dr. Bright, a doctor she knew from where she worked. So they bundled me up and took me. The doctor took one look at me and took my temperature, which was 107.6 degrees. He said "Meet me at the hospital. I'm taking him with me". I was in Moore White Medical Center for the next three weeks. My right ear was infected all the way to the inner eardrum. It cooked my brain and burnt it black. This caused me to be paralyzed on my right side completely. I had to learn to use my left side again. So now I am known as a lefty. I had to go to seeing, hearing, speech and coordination therapy three or four times a week. Mom would take me to the morning sessions and Dad took me to the afternoon ones. We had Kaiser Insurance, so all of the doctors were in the same building. When I was four years old, I started to get my speech back. At first it was just jabber, but within a few months, I was very understandable.

At the age of five, mom enrolled me in Hollywood Professional School. I did very well there. The bad part of it was a teacher that would read a book to us. When asked about what the story was, I would tell them word for word. I could not read any of it, but instead memorized the whole story. Mom had to hire a reading tutor so I could catch up to the other students.

At the age of seven, my brother, Brother Topcop said I should go to Lee-Way "special school" for slow students that have physical problems. I went and I loved it! They helped me with my coordination and hearing a lot. My teacher at Lee-Way told my mom that I should take piano lessons for my hand therapy and take me bowling for my foot therapy. Mom did just that, and I became more stable on my feet and got where I could use my right hand a lot more. I learned to help mom out around the house. I could dust all of the shelves, vacuum the rugs, and wash a few dishes. Dad was in and out of the hospital a lot of the time. Mom worked and took care of dad, so I said I wanted to help her as much as I could. She let me because it also helped me. When dad was in the hospital, I went to work with her. I liked that. Everyone she worked with, including her boss, liked me and treated me like a prince. I was almost 10 years old when my dad went to the hospital and had to stay because his condition [leukemia] had worsened. My sister was in the Army, stationed in one of the southern states in the US. She got a special leave to come home to see dad. She stayed for a week. She wanted us to move to the city her military base was located in if dad died. He died December 24, 1980 at 9 P.M. We were at my Uncle God's Toy's for a Christmas party. Mom only took me because dad took me every year since I was five months old. We never missed a year going. It was great. We had a Santa Clause and a lot of gifts, plus a lot of good things to eat. The entire family would be there. Uncle God's Toy was a retired narc. He was captain of the Narcotics Squad of Hollywood Division. He always told me to say no to drugs. Go back to when I was seven years old. I had to go to work with mom. She was working a political function at the Hollywood Paladium. The function was a fund raiser for Barry Goldwater to run for President of the United States of America. Ronald Reagan and Nancy Reagan were there. He was the Governor of California at the time. I overheard Mrs. Reagan telling Mrs. Goldwater that she had to speak at an elementary school where the kids were very young. She did not know how or what she would tell them about drugs. I went over to her and asked her if I could help her. Mrs. Reagan asked me, "Where did you come from? Who are you here with?" I told her my mother was one of the ladies serving the event.

I pointed to mom and said that was the one. I told her to tell the kids to "Just say no and no means no." Ronald Reagan liked that and turned around and shook my hand. Mrs. Reagan said, "I will use that statement. I like it." This is how the slogan "Just say no" got started. It helped alot of young people decide not to use drugs. It is being used everyday. I did not know who the Reagan's were at the time. After I had spoke with the First Lady, Mom was let go, before dessert was even served. It was still early so mom and I went and visited dad in the hospital. When I got home mom told me he was the Governor and First Lady of California. The phone was ringing and it was mom's supervisor. He apologized for letting her go and said that he had spoke with the Reagans and that they said it was understandable, under mom's conditions, that she had brought me to work with her in the first place. He rehired her over the phone and she hung up. Mom told me to forget about the meeting for now and go do my homework and get to bed. When I was eight, mom's hours at work changed a bit. She had to be at work at three in the morning. Holiday Inn got a contract to serve the recruits joining the military. She had to be there to cook and set-up the buffet for 50 or so people. She would call me at seven am to wake me up. She set-up my breakfast and made me a lunch before she left for work. I would get dressed and eat then catch the bus. I would get home about an hour before she got home. She had won a new lawn mower in a contest. I didn't know how to use it. My bus driver asked if I wanted him (Mr. Bernie) to teach me how to use it. Since I was the last student off the bus he would spend time helping mow the grass. He helped me learn how to put clothes in washing machine and to hang them on the cloths line to dry. Mom invited Mr. Bernie and his wife out to dinner. We all had a great time. We went to El

Rosas, a Mexican restaurant. After dinner we all went bowling at Mr. T's.

We became good friends. Then summer came and I didn't go to school. I didn't see Mr. Bernie for three months. I had to start going to work with mom. She would get me up at 2 a.m. every day. She had a room at the hotel that she'd put me to bed in. Her boss let us use it so I could get my rest. I'd get up about eight and go down and have breakfast. I would help mom and the other waitresses clean up after breakfast and setup for the lunch group. I loved to go to work with mom. I was learning something new every day. When I had my ninth birthday, the crew at the Holiday Inn gave me a great party. It was a big surprise for me. When we left work, mom took the cake with us. She had set it up with the hospital to get the visitors room for us. When we got there my dad was sitting in a wheelchair and my brother and all my aunts and uncles were there. Boy was this a big party. I was really surprised and happy. We had food brought in for everybody. Dad ate really good and had a piece of cake. I was so happy. I think this was the best day of my life. A plus was I received good stuff plus a lot of money. I have really enjoyed this summer. I'm going shopping this weekend for school clothes and supplies I need. I was ready to go back to school. I missed my friends. We went on day trips to a lot of places such as Famous Amos Cookie Plant, the zoo, the La Brea Tar Pits, and the Hollywood Police Headquarters. We went to Movie Studio and met Don Knotts of the Andy Griffith show. We met a lot more stars while we were there. We got to go to the Glendale Mall and have lunch once a week. This was always a fun trip. There would be 10 or 12 of us students at a time.

I still had to have therapy for my coordination and the use of my right leg, but I was getting a lot better at doing things.

Mom could not be home when I got home from school. She set up a deal with the owner of Mr. T's Bowling Alley that I would be allowed to bowl four or five games and have a snack from the snack bar. She would pay for it when she came to pick me up. It was only two blocks from our house. This worked out great for both of us. She knew where I was when she was not home and I had a good time. She made the same deal with the movie house. I could see a movie and have a snack. She would come get me and pay. Then we would go see my dad.

School is out for the summer and my sister, Sister Cowgirl, wants me to come to Exeter, Missouri to visit her. Mom said if I wanted to, I could go for two months. She raised greyhound dogs to race. She also had horses, cows, and chickens on her ranch. I loved to ride horses and take care of them. I would take them down to the creek to give them a bath and bring them back to the barn so I could brush them. I loved the ranch life.

I spent my 10th birthday at Sister Cowgirl's. I had a good time with Archie and her two kids. I helped take care of Princess and Mr. Chambers. Princess was six and Mr. Chambers was three. I taught them how to tie their shoes. Archie could not understand how they learned to tie them left-handed instead of right-handed. It was not easy, but they learned. I'll be going home tomorrow. I'll be happy to see mom and dad. I've missed them. Mom will meet me at the airport and take me to visit dad.

Dad was not doing too well. The doctor had to give him a pint of blood twice a day. Mom and my family would donate blood for him every four to five weeks. It was enough we didn't have to pay for any of the blood. I started back to school the next week. We had finished doing the shopping for clothes and school supplies.

We had to buy a lot because none of my clothes would fit me now. Mom said I had grown three inches since last year. I had slimmed down since I had worked at the ranch. I started school today. It was so nice to see my friends and teachers. My classes were different now. I had therapy along with my class work. My instructors were surprised and happy to see that I had made great progress with running, talking, and hearing. I had done a lot of practice on my vacation and it worked out well for me. I still had to overcome my handicaps and disabilities. I knew I was winning. I'm still going to work with mom. Her boss, Mr. Harry, gave me a uniform that fit me. I thought I was a real employee. I served coffee and water to the customers, who appeared to enjoy it. I really enjoyed helping the waitresses. I learned how to bus and set the tables for the next guests. I still go to Ravens bar, pizza bowling alley every day. I'm on a league with eight teams now. We're in fourth place, but are trying to get better. All the boys and girls on the league had a disability or handicap. We bowl every Saturday morning. The league was called Young Bowlers of the United States. I received a plaque for Most Improved Bowler for my 11th birthday. Mom set up a party with all the league bowlers. We had hot dogs, hamburgers, fries, and drinks. We bowled four games each. We had a small prize for different pins to be knocked down. Each one of us won at least one prize. Then we had a cake that was shaped like a bowling pin. We left and took dad a piece of cake. I showed him my prize and he sat up and talked to mom for a while. He told us how much he loved us and missed us. Mom wanted to take him home with us for awhile, but the doctor said "no." He had to be there to get his blood treatment. Otherwise, he could go into a comatose state. He was getting up to four pints of blood a day at this time. Auntie Alison. called while we were at the hospital visiting. She talked to dad and asked to speak to me. She wanted us to come by their house on the way home. She got me a lot of clothes for my birthday. Since school will start in a couple of weeks, I needed them. I know that I'm the most loved kid in the whole world. My family shows me every day just how much I am cherished. I love all of them with all my heart.

I'm going to stay the weekend with my friend, Juan. He and his family live in Pomano. He used to live next door to us until his father was transferred to a different location after receiving a new position within his company.

I start back to school in two days. I'll be glad to get back to my normal routine and seeing my many friends at school. I missed them all summer. My first day back was great. I still had two of my teachers from last year. I love math and history. I don't care much about English and literature. Too much writing. I do not have the same bus driver. Ms. Evans is okay, but I liked Mr. Bernie because he would help me learn things I should know.

Mom and I are going to visit dad today. I have not been in three days. He hasn't been alert. He's going in and out of a coma state. When we left to go home, mom said that I would have to go see him every day with her. We went by Auntie Alison and Uncle Master Pool Shark's house. Mom talked to them in the den. I played board games with my cousin, Jack. Jack having the advantage of being 16 and myself only being 11, I could never win. He was good at the games. When we played checkers, I beat him every time. I was an expert at checkers. I always played dad. He taught me so well that I even started to beat him.

Auntie Alison called and invited us for Thanksgiving dinner. We went and the entire family was there. I never knew that I had so many people related to me. My cousin, Pleasant Boyd, was the greatest cook in the world. She cooked for parties of three or four hundred guests. She would cook every day for a month. All of our family would always end up at her house for the holidays. We would always get there early so we could help put the food out. Pleasant Boyd had a big house. It was like a mansion. It was a big white house just below the observatory in Hollywood. We took some food to dad. He loves Pleasant Boyd's cooking. He didn't eat much, but he enjoyed us being there with him. We stayed about an hour. Mom had to get home and put laundry in the machine. We still had not replaced the dryer, so we took them to the laundry mat to dry them.

Well, back to school for me. This was a long weekend. Next month is Christmas and we will be out of school for 12 days. Mom is already helping Pleasant Boyd prepare food and freeze it for the party. She'll have about 300 guests of family, friends, and priests. She always has two priests from church at her party. She always has the party on the 19th of December. Uncle Fred Pool Shark has the basement setup just like a pool room. He is teaching me to play pool. He says I'm getting pretty good. He is the greatest pool player there is. He puts pool tournaments on every year for the Elks Club. He does trick shots for television shows all the time. The one I liked best was for "Love American Style" and also for the movie "Sting." By the way, Fred is known as "Freddie the Thief Famous Gangster."

We are on our way to the Christmas party. The men go to the basement and play pool. They were competing for $1000 a ball and $5000 for the 8-ball. This is where I met a great player known as "Minnesota Fats." He bet me a dollar. I won. He said that he'd give me five dollars if I didn't tell Uncle Master Pool Shark. Uncle Master Pool Shark found out and he told Fats "I overheard that my nephew beat you, why don't we let him make the 8-ball in for me". I was getting ready to shoot when Uncle Master Pool Shark said "hold on, why we don't raise the stakes to $10,000". I looked at him and said "Uncle Master Pool Shark, you're killing me". He said "if you scratch or miss, then I will". I made it and Uncle Master Pool Shark gave me $50, but Fats never did pay me the original five dollars. The party was great and everyone had a good time.

We have to leave early because mom has to go to work at three o'clock. I have to go to work with her. She'll get off work about 2 P.M. and go see dad before we go home. I told him all about the party and how well I played pool. He told me I was getting better at all the things I do. He said I was "the man of the house" until he could get back home. He told me how proud of me he was. He said that I was growing up to be a fine and up-standing young man. My brother, Topcop, and his wife just got here to visit. So Mom said we'd go. We left and stopped to get some dinner before we went home.

Uncle God's Toy had called to ask if we'd come to his Christmas party on the 24th of December. Dad took me to their house for Christmas every year since I was a baby. Mom said she couldn't because she had to work, and then go see my Dad. He and Topcop said, "Wunderlich has never missed the party in his life. If you will bring him, we will go and spend the whole day visiting father on Christmas day." She said she would come, but we had to leave early.

We got to the party at 8 P.M. It was already swinging. Uncle God's Toy had a Santa there for us kids. There were about 20 of us. He gave each of us a present. Mine was a camera. My Uncle's God's Toy wife was the best Mexican cook. We had the best Mexican food ever. She was Mexican. Uncle God's Toy was a retired captain on the

Narc's of California. My brother, Topcop, was a narcotics agent of Los Angeles Police Department. So, you see I grew up hating drugs. They all told me if I was accused of anything and I was innocent they would stand with me all the way. But if I was in the wrong, I'd have to answer to the problem myself. Mom raised me with the rule of consequences. She said she had taught me right from wrong. But as I would go through life, I would see some things I'd like to do that were wrong. If I wanted to do whatever, I should stop and weigh the consequences and if I thought I was man enough to pay the penalty for it, go ahead and do it... but don't call her. This kept me from getting into trouble.

We just got home from the party. It is 11 P.M. and we have to get to bed so we can get to work at 3 A.M. I had just got to sleep when I was awaked by dad. He came and sat on the side of my bed. He said, "I have to go now. Please get a good education and always take care of your mother. You are the man of the house now. I'll see you when you get to heaven." I ran and jumped in mom's bed. I told her that dad was here and had just left. At that time, the phone rang. Mom answered it. Her boss was on the line telling her to call the hospital and leave a number where we could be reached. Dad had died at 9 P.M. Topcop had forgotten to call and leave a phone number where he would be, so mom called Uncle God's Toy and told him that father had passed away. My brother was still there. Mom talked to him. She said she has to go to work at 3 that morning and had no one she could call to take care of the inductees. She would come to the hospital a few hours later around 7 A.M. Topcop told her he would go and take care of things himself. Dad had in his will that he wanted to be cremated. Topcop got the arrangements set up for her. We went to the hospital to get his personal belongings and be there when they came for him. This was the worst Christmas I had ever had. Topcop said we would all come to his house for a wake. Dad was cremated on December 27, 1980. Mom gave his ashes to Topcop to spread at sea. I told Auntie Alison about Dad coming and sitting on the side of my bed the night he died. She said that was because he loved me more than anything in the world. I knew he did because I loved him, and was very sad that I'd never see him again. My sister, Sister Cowgirl, is here for the wake. She wants us to come live in Missouri. She will give us two acres (out of the 140 acres she owns) to build on, but mom declines because she said she has a job and that we will be fine. My sister, Sister Relative, wants us to move to the city her base is located. She says we need to have our family together. I don't really want to move, however. I like my school that and Uncle Master Pool Shark and Auntie Alison and all the rest of the Famous Gangster and Wunderlich clan is located nearby.

Auntie Alison passed away on April 10, 1981. I did not get to go to the memorial for her. Mom had a meeting at work. I went to work with her because she did not know how long it would last. Her friends at work prayed for mom and told her they loved her.

Pleasant Boyd is putting the house on the market to sell. Both Uncle Master Pool Shark and Pleasant Boyd said since Eric retired from N.A.S.A. they were going to buy a home in Sisters, Oregon. John, her oldest son, already has a home there. Mom said if they move to Oregon, we will let Sister Relative find us a house near her military base. I'll be out of school for the summer in June.

I'll have my 12th birthday in July. I'm the man of the house now. I told mom that we would be better off moving closer to my sister because she will make sure we are a family. Mom started to sell what we didn't need that way we had less to move across the country. We got a Hertz rent-a-truck and started out on our trip. We let a nice couple have our house. Our former land lady said she would accept them to finish out our lease. We stayed our last two nights in Los Angeles at the Holiday Inn. Mom's boss gave us a transfer to the Holiday Inn to our hometown. We left on August 15, and took a scenic tour on the way. It was a fantastic trip. Sister Relative had found us a beautiful 3-bedroom home. It was three blocks from the school I was going to be attending. I did not like the idea that I would need to get booster shots before I could go to school. But that was the state law here. We arrived in our new residence on August 19.

After we got settled in, mom decided to go to Florida to see some family and friends. I had never met any of her side of the family. It was a great trip. Her brother John's wife, Betty, cooked fried oysters, fried mullet fish, and something called "swamp cabbage." It was all kinds of new food for me. But it was very good. It was really nice to meet my uncles, aunts, and all my cousins that I had never met. We left Uncle John's and went to the cemetery. Mom showed me my grandmother's and great- grandmother's gravesites. There were a lot of graves that belonged to our family. We went to several houses to visit when we left the cemetery. Then, we had to leave because it was a six hour drive back home. Sister Relative and I slept most of the way back. We stopped in a small town to fuel up and get a snack. I tried my first ever boiled peanuts there. I loved them. When we got home, I was ready for a shower and a good night's sleep. Sister Relative had to go back to base. She had duty the next morning.

Today is the first day of school. I had never been to a public school before. Prior to now, I had been enrolled in private schools in California. It was very hard at first to adjust because I was a little slower at learning than the other pupils. I became good friends with some of the students. They would come to my house after school and help me with my class work. It didn't take long before I was doing very well in my classes. I really enjoyed not being in a special school anymore.

I was asked to be the Chairman for Local toy charity this year. I had collected a lot of toys and money for the kids. I was on a bowling team at Garden City Bowling Alley. We had a bowling event for Local toy charity. I won first place which is the reason I was asked to be the chairman. When we were supposed to be on television, it was cancelled. We had a big fire downtown in a historical home at that time. No one was injured, which was the good part. But the house could not be saved. I was still a guest of the Marines. I got to help deliver the toys with them.

We had made no plans for Thanksgiving dinner. Mom had to work, so we thought we would have dinner at a restaurant on the way home. Boy, what a surprise! Nothing was open... not even a fast food place. We did not know that all places close on holidays. We ended up going to a 7-11 store and getting hotdogs and chips. Mom asked the clerk about everything being closed and he replied, "that was just the way it was." My sister, Sister Cowgirl, wants us to come spend Christmas with her. Sister Relative said she could not go because she had duty. The only day she could be off was Christmas day. But of course, mom had to work that day. But we would have loved for her to come here during the holidays. She couldn't come because she has all the animals to take care of there. Mom said I could visit her for a week. I got there by bus. Sister Cowgirl met me there. I love her ranch. She has 40 greyhound dogs that she races.

We had two winners at the track the first day I got there. She also has six horses we can ride as well as 12 Clydesdales horses that she raised for the Budweiser Company. These horses are huge. I was afraid of them at first, but I got use to them. I would feed them and brush them. I'm going home tomorrow. Mom will meet me at the bus station. I was glad to get home. It was a long ride back. My sister, Sister Relative, came over and had dinner. She said she missed me and wanted to know all about my trip. I told her about the snow and how cold it was. I talked about the dogs and the horses. I told her that Sister Cowgirl wants me to come up on summer vacation. Mom said it was up to me as long as I kept my grades up. I was doing well in school. I wasn't a brain storm, but I did manage to keep a B-grade average, which was good for me.

New Year's Eve is next week. Mom wants to go to a party. She has a friend now and I said it was alright with me. I'll have some of my bowling friends coming for a sleepover. Dwight and Kim are brother and sister. Heather will be here as a chaperone. Mom put all the food and trimmings out for us. Mom and the other parents called us at 12 midnight to wish us all Happy New Years and tell all of us how much they loved us. Mom got home at 1 am and told all of us to go to bed. And we did. The next morning she woke us up for breakfast and then we took my friends home. Everything was going great. Mom was working two jobs and putting food on the table and a roof over our heads. We always had what we needed and some things we wanted. I was going to school and doing household chores and yard work. Mom received a letter from the landlord asking us to move because her family members were coming home soon. We started packing to move and found a home closer to my high school. At my new high school, Orchard Academy, I loved it. It was the best school in the area. I made new friends there and I still had my best friends Kim and Dwight that I still bowl with every Saturday morning in the Young Bowlers of the United States. We are going to the state capitol for a bowling tournament. I would go to a different city every year for a state bowling tournament.

Mom's boss wants me to clean the swimming pool at the hotel every week. She pays me for doing odd jobs for her. She believed that as long as you kept busy that you wouldn't get into trouble. I fully agreed, besides, I liked to have my own money. I can buy presents for mom without her knowing what I was getting her.

School is getting harder, my literature is real bad because I didn't understand the southern drawl of some of the teachers. I went home with a D and mom was disappointed with me. When I explained to her the teacher's dialect, she understood after meeting one of my teachers in the grocery store. Mom hired a tutor, which was a teacher that worked with her in the hotel. Mom asked him what he could do to help me and he said he would come over to the house to help me. Every Monday and Friday nights. His name was Luke. He taught me to enjoy reading and learning and mom would cook him dinner and also do his laundry. Luke helped me with all my subjects so I could maintain a B average. I'm going to the 11th grade next year. I worked all summer and mom started demonstrating products at the grocery stores. She got me a job demo-ing as well, and boy, I loved that job. Mom and I would compete who could sell the most products. Sometimes I would win because I had a better product. I had an honor that was given to me the next week, dressing up as Mr. Oreo for the kids coming in the store and mom did the chubby checker twist. She would have a stacking oreo contest, giving cookie samples. I did not care for my oreo suit. It was hot but I liked it when the kids would come over and give me a big hug. Of course, some of the real small ones were afraid of me. They still wanted the cookies though.

I joined the Junior Reserve Officer Training Corps at school. This kept me busy. We had to go to all kinds of functions such as all the home sports games and theatre specials like the opera and skits. We marched in parades and city and school activities.

In my senior year, 1989, I had two courses of J.R.O.T.C. I used one period to do my homework. I needed an extra credit so I could graduate. I made it and graduated with a B+ average. I went to the prom with a friend of mine. She looked fantastic, but she's not the girl for me. I was not interested in a serious relationship at this time. Mom and some other parents got together and planned a graduation party for us after the walk down the aisle to get our sheep skin paper. We had dinner and danced till 1 am. We had about 60 people at the party. It was the first unchaperoned event I had been to.

I got a job at Famous Steakhouse. I was a bus boy. I liked the job. Lisa was the owner and manager. When she asked me to be the host and cashier, I was thrilled to death. This meant more money, and I enjoyed meeting the customers. Lisa talked to me about college. I told her I could not afford it at this time, but was working on saving for it. She said I could get a pell grant and a loan so I could start going to college and so I started going to Phillips College. Lisa's daughter was going there and she was studying nursing. I signed up for computer classes. I loved it. I was fascinated about computers anyway. Mom said I could live at home and didn't have to pay any rent. We would take my paycheck every week and pay the student loan. Then I would have most of it paid off and not have to pay as much when I graduated. That was a good idea because the college went broke and closed their doors. I had only been going there a year and no one graduated that year. This caused a huge uproar from the people in this town after the college closed. I had my student loan paid off in six months. Lisa would let me use her computer in the office and I would also go into the public library to use their computers to continue learning about computers. I was hopeful that I could get a job working with computers but unfortunately I wasn't experienced enough to get a job. So I got a job working in a convenience store. And during the summer I would do two jobs and I was able to pay off my loan. I took mom out for dinner and took her to the place I worked. Ms. Lisa was the owner of the Famous Steakhouse and she would not let me pay for my dinner but I insisted on paying for moms. Mom said she wanted to find a home we could afford to buy and she saved all the money dad left us and also his insurance money. So we went looking and found a few we liked but not exactly what we wanted. I talked to a man at the convenience store where I worked and he told me about a real estate agent and gave me his phone number. I gave it to mom. She called him and he told her he was working on a house that would be ready in a couple months. Mom said that was good because with the holidays coming up she did not have time for all the things she needed to do to buy a home or not to sell it. Our lease where we lived was not up until April 1st. The real estate agent said that would be perfect. We went to see the house and liked what we saw and we signed the paperwork in early 1996. He said we could go ahead and start hanging curtains or whatever we wanted to do in the house. We bought all new appliances plus an air conditioner. It was really starting to look good. Mom bought me a big workshed for all my tools, and it was HUGE! It was 16' x 18'. This was an all American dream we had. We moved in on April 4, 1996. We had a small party on the weekend for our open house. My sister and a few friends came over. It felt good to own our own home. We got four rose bushes from our guests. The next day I planted them. They are beautiful.

We were in our new home about a week and our neighbor came and introduced himself. He said his name was Jack. We thought he was just being neighborly and friendly. He was not. He warned us that he sold drugs and had prostitutes of all ages next door and if we didn't like it, we could move or he would have some of his "young bucks" come and take care of us. I asked him to leave. He turned around and said, "If you white people cause me any problems, I, and my bucks will gang rape your mom as you watch and set the house on fire with you inside". That same night they were shooting at someone. We called the sheriff's department but the officer could not find the person that was shot or being shot at. We found out that Jack was a convicted felon for murder and on parole now. He has 20 to 25 drug runners on the street behind our house. We live on Hell Street, but there is no parking out front because the street is so narrow. The sidewalk is right outside our front door, so we only have one way in our house which is from Teflon Street (behind our house). We had a driveway into our backyard. Next door had drug parties with a lot of smoking joints and using crack. A fight broke out and gunshots were heard. We called the law. The sheriff came and busted them. They arrested at least 16 people. All the others ran and got away. The neighbor we had met earlier came over the next morning and warned us that we were in his area and that we better not call the law again. The law always believed them when they said they didn't do what we had said they had done. There were more of them denying the accusations versus just me and mom.

Mom said we would start showing the law the truth. She went to Toys-R-Us and bought a baby camera. She had a man build a dog house for us. She told him it was special and wanted a door with a place to put a lock on it in the front and a hole in the backboard about two inches in diameter. We had to learn to set the camera up and get electricity into it without the extension cord being seen going into the dog house. March 17, 1997; our next door neighbor decides to have one of his drug users file a charge of indecent exposure against me. Mom had to come down to the jail and bail me out. It took eight whole hours for me to get out. Our real estate agent came over and told us that the same neighbor we have been having issues with wanted to buy the house next door, on the other side of us. He knew the problems we were having with the other tenant and all of his "young bucks". Mom asked him if we could buy that house the same way we had bought this house. Mom did not want to get boxed in with drug dealers on every side of us. Our real estate agent said he would get the paperwork done in the next couple days. This made the neighbor even more furious than he already was. He had a female friend file another charge against me because she said I had pulled my pants down in front of her kids. Mom had to come bail me out, again. When we got home from jail, Jack came over to the fence and told us that this was just the start of things to come. I finally got the camera set up in the backyard pointing at the gate. We had a monitor in the sitting room, that way we could see and hear everything that they were saying or doing next door from our house. I was charged once again by a different friend of Jack. He stated that I called him racial names and the sheriff's department charged me with disorderly conduct. He owned a gun shop where coincidentally our infamous neighbor, his "young bucks", and law enforcement bought their guns and ammo. This charge was dismissed due to the video evidence proving my innocence. One day, Jack came over and asked why we had a dog house when we didn't even have a dog. I went and got a dog, a black lab. I named her Loni Anderson because she was so beautiful.

Mom said we needed some privacy because they could look over the fence and see everything we did. We got Manor Lumber Company to come put up a six foot privacy fence between our yard and the yard next to us. The back fence gate was the only wire part. Jack proceeded to have his "young bucks" sit on the roof of his house so they could see over the fence and know when the law was coming. Every time we would go out the back door his "young bucks" would insult us and threaten us. We were going out the back gate one day when the neighbor came over to the car and told my mom they wouldn't hurt her because she was a mother, but would take me out. Mom told him, "If you touch Wunderlich, just remember I live next door to you and I have my guns and the knowledge of how to make a molotov cocktail, so you and your family would not be safe living next door to me". This was an American dream turned into a nightmare from Hell. We had to live here because we could not get out of the contract at this time. We got the first two charges against me dismissed. I thought this would be the end of it, but unfortunately, it was not! We bought the house on our other side from our real estate agent and rented it out to a young lady that was pregnant. She worked at the state mental hospital and she was a student. Jack got a hold of her and propositioned her to make more money by not paying us rent and by selling drugs for him. She moved her boyfriend into her house to sell drugs with her. He started to physically abuse her and soon after caused her to lose the baby. I and mom went to the funeral.

After we evicted her for three months non-payment of rent, I went into the house and found extensive damage to the walls. I took pictures of the damages and went to court. The judge ordered her to pay me $475 but she never paid me. I went over and was trying to fix the damages when I decided to just board up the house. I was furious at the situation. Jack's son-in-law was his personal drug supplier. The son-in-law came over one night and knocked on our back door. When we answered, he pulled a gun on us. After making numerous racial threats, he went out the gate, closed the gate, and said "if you do have a camera up, then take a picture of this" and pulled his pants down and exposed himself in front of the camera. Mom called the law. She showed the video to the officer and he refused to see it. Mom told the officer "if you don't look at it, I will take it directly to the solicitor's office". She left and went to the solicitor's office and met with Solicitor Sherry. She and her office viewed the video and they charged the son-in-law with indecent exposure and disorderly conduct.

We were asked to join the Orchard County Republican Party. We saw that most of the corruption we were fighting was Democrats. We were very outspoken and even taped signs on the car, bumper stickers, and glass paint. With glass paint, we painted our own messages. Our good friend, Ms. Intellect, would buy tickets to campaign dinners and always invited us. Our friend Congressman would pay our way to all conventions and galas. Our city's mayor, whom we helped get elected twice, always made sure we had tickets to any political functions that were happening.

We were so outspoken that the political parties nicknamed us the "Wunderlich political machine". We learned from the best on grass roots; Ms. Intellect and the mayor. We went door to door with literature and talked to the people. The chairman of the Republican Party was amazed at the extent we were politically outspoken.

I was asked to go as a guest to Victory Baptist Church by an officer of Orchard County. I was rebaptized and many of the people became our friends at the church. We started going to community meetings and talked about our drug dealing neighbors and the abuse of the children.

We were asking for help from elected officials and churches. I even went to the Nation of Islam mosque and I told them I come in peace and I was invited into their shrine. They listened to me when I told them about the problems stemming from Jack and the others, the raping of young children, the drug dealing, and about the children. The Nation of Islam started walking the neighborhood with lead pipes and baseball bats, trying to help us clean up the neighborhood. After a while they started to have vandalism to their shrine and their cars, so they had to move them out of the area. We started writing tags of the cars that were going next door and we also called the schools security, giving them the descriptions of the drug runners. We also observed people going next door and using their food stamps to buy drugs and the children prostitutes. We wrote letters to the governor at the time and the Attorney General at the time. We told them about the people and how they were using food stamps for our next door neighbor's services. The state changed from paper food stamps to the EBT cards we use today.

Jack's brother-in-law, before getting arrested, was cited for not stopping at a stop sign. He tried using another name when the officer had a warrant issued... My mom told the officer that he is the one, we don't care what name he is trying to use. He was arrested that night. We let the Solicitor Sherry watch the video and listen to a part of the tape when Jack's brother-in-law was bragging to his family and friends about killing a man at "the mud hole" (a name for a drug house). Solicitor Sherry ended up dropping mom's case, for a murder charge. The officers under Orchard County's sheriff order would not watch our videos anymore. Jack was pulled over on his way home and was charged with a DUI. They tested him at our back gate and took him to jail. When he came home, he was very angry and started making threats. His strong man said he would have me and my mom dead. We called the law and had him arrested. Jack kept trying to bail him out but he couldn't. We went to court and the Assistant Magistrate said 200 dollars cash bond. With aggression and anger, Jack's strong man exposed himself in the holding cell and completely tore up the holding cell. The Assistant Magistrate said he wanted an additional 1,000 dollars cash bond for the damages and contempt of court. He got out in 30 days but soon got arrested for shoplifting at a paint store. We went to court and the Assistant Magistrate took one look at the offender and said "bond REVOKED! you will stay in jail until you go before another judge". Jack kept having drug and Raping parties almost every night. A man came down one day and asked the neighbor what my name was. He told him, R. Wunderlich. The two men had worked together on cars on their properties. The business partner drove a tow truck and he would tow cars to his house. Many of them were stolen and he would strip them and then take them somewhere. We started getting the tag numbers with the descriptions of the cars and reporting them. We found out from an officer that a car had been reported stolen two days ago. The neighbor's business partner went with another guy to have as his witness and charged me with disorderly conduct. I was at the bowling alley and when I had got home, the business partner called his friend that, come to find out, was an officer, and told him to come arrest me because he had just got a warrant for me. The officer came to my house and took me into custody before the warrant had been processed. That was a violation of my rights. Mom came and bailed me out and we got home around 4 am in the morning. I started writing letters to one of Orchard County's District Attorney Livingstone. I told the District Attorney Livingstone he was doing a good job and told him about people using phony names to the officers. He wrote me back and told me we need more honest citizens like me. HA! within a week of our letters, I was summoned for jury duty. I was sent home though because they had plea bargained the case. I wrote letters to all the elected officials in Orchard County and the state. We went to court and showed Solicitor Sherry a newspaper article, stating that Jack's friend, Miles was arrested and indicted. Solicitor Sherry had us in one room and Jack and his business partner in another. She left us and went into the other room. Jack's business partner wanted to switch Jack for one of his friends, she said NO. The case will be dismissed. Thank God we had one honest, decent prosecutor in office. They didn't realize that the case had to go to court to be dismissed and that the court date had to be set. The duo from next door were so angry that the charge was dismissed that they went into the Chief's office and complained that every time they charged me, I would get out in a couple of hours. The chief said that they needed to charge me with a felony, charge things like terroristic threats and acts. He suggested they take pictures of my property which was a violation of the privacy act and get petitions signed by the neighbors. A lot of the neighbors refused to sign it so the two men started forging phony names on it. They took the information the chief requested. He assigned the case to Investigator Fallow, who called me and left messages on my answering machine; we began playing phone tag. I finally said jokingly, "tag, you're it! I'm a leprechaun, catch me if you can." Investigator Fallow took it seriously. When we finally set an interview at my house he brought another investigator with him. We knew the second investigator prior to this because we tried to get him to watch the famous tape of Jack's brother-in-law bragging about killing some guy. He never watched it. Investigator Fallow was surprised that we knew the investigator that was accompanying him. The Investigator Fallow was very rude and disrespectful to us. He never told us why he was there and what I was suspected of doing. Mom got tired of him being rude to me and asked him why he was here. He said, "I have a couple of complaints from your neighbors about Wunderlich". She asked what the complaints were. He said "You need to shut up and go into another part of the house. I'm not here to talk to you." I said, "Wait a minute, you and your partner are a guest in our home, you can leave right now". As they were leaving, the Investigator Fallow opened his car door and mom asked him again what the complaints were. He said "Wunderlich threatened to blow up the block and kill everyone". This charge, they knew, was bogus. Our home, property, and she were not checked by the bomb squad, ATF, GBI, or FBI. Before they had come to our house for this lovely visit, mom had noticed that they had been next door, and she knew there was something wrong here. She told me to go ahead with the interview and get the tape recorder. We advised them of the recorder. Both of the investigators agreed that we could record their interview. After they left and we closed the door, mom called the chief to complain about the disrespectful treatment and he replied that she better find me a lawyer and make sure he's a good one. And then he hung up.

When I was indicted, I was in the house next to us fixing up the damages. They came to the house with my mother and handcuffed me and put me into a patrol car. No Miranda warning given. My mother told me to say nothing to them, because they were not following the law. She asked the officers when she could come down and bail me out of jail and the officer replied, "You know the routine, you can come down in four to six hours, and oh, by the way, this is a felony and there might not be a bond". I spent 45 days in jail; they denied me any bail until I had a mental evaluation. My mother was told by Chief Judge "you better hire him a lawyer". She replied "he has a lawyer, Mr. D. When mom got home, she started calling all past and present elected officials, trying to get me a bond. Rep. Torro and Rep. Zingler started working on my mental evaluation. Since Rep. Torro was a big man on the board of the mental hospital, he had the hospital send a doctor to the jail, since the mental hospital had no available room for me and the other people waiting for mental evaluations. My mother found out from the jail that there were at least ten other guys who had all been locked up for six months to a year, all waiting for mental evaluations. Thanks to Rep. Torro, we all got our evaluations and were released on bond. He also ensured that a doctor routinely visited the jail to conduct mental evaluations, so that this would not happen again. The court tries to justify themselves with unreasonable incarcerations by ordering mental evaluations, violating citizen's constitutional and civil rights to a speedy trial.

While I was incarcerated, mom found out my cell doors and others didn't lock and so she had me moved to another cell block while they fixed the doors. I became the houseman in charge of taking dirty laundry and handing out clean laundry, store call and giving supplies to new inmates. I made a lot of friends and they protected me from the baby killer (our previous rentee's boyfriend). They threatened him with taking him to the second floor and dropping him to the first floor. He smarted off to THE BOSS, who was the leader of seven people who were gangsters from somewhere up north. THE BOSS spoke up and said "we will pick you up and take you upstairs you baby killer". I had just done a favor for THE BOSS, writing a letter for his driver. After I wrote the letter to the judge, I found out that the driver couldn't read or write, so I stated my name and put into the letter his inability to read or write. Honorable Judge Halter asked who wrote this letter for him. He replied "a fellow inmate wrote the letter for me". Judge Halter spoke up and said "I know Mr. Wunderlich wrote this letter for you. I am offering you an opportunity to learn to read and write. You can come to my office every Wednesday and I will teach you". Then he ordered his release from jail. The driver came running towards me, hugging and thanking me. He said "I am going home today!" In the letter I put that he would volunteer at his church and take care of his sick mother and wife. I was scheduled to go before the Honorable Judge Halter the following week to have the third charges dismissed. He said, "Mr. Wunderlich, you are a good and honest man, I wish you the best of luck". I had written a letter for my mother and asked the solicitor's assistant to hand it to my mother. He said "NO, I don't work for you". Judge Halter spoke up and said "Mr. Wunderlich, you may hand the letter to your mother". I gave her the letter, and a kiss, and said "I love you mom". I started crying. As I was leaving the courtroom, I said thank you to Judge Halter.

I was the checkers champion of my cell block. Mom would come visit me every visitation day. When I finally got a bond set, the judge and District Attorney Livingstone made an order. My attorney told mom over the phone that we have two days to move or my bond would be revoked. Mom said that would be impossible because her being in a wheelchair, there was no way to move that fast. Mr. D. said "let me talk to the judge and see what I can do, your camera has to come down NOW, as soon as we hang up". He called us back soon thereafter and said that we had thirty days to move, starting now. That night we heard a window in the living room being pushed up. Mom had me put 4 inch nails above each window. The intruder had taken the screen off the window. Mom opened the curtain, locked and cocked her pistol, and started tapping the window with it right between his eyes, while I was begging her not to shoot him. He finally noticed the gun and jumped off the porch, straddling the fence. On the fence, we had a wild rose bush with very long thorns. It went between his legs and he ran down the street screaming like Festus on Gun smoke.

We started packing and looking for a place to move. We found one, a shack of a rundown trailer that was about 15 minutes away in Woods County, in the middle of the woods. While we were moving, our car caught on fire under the hood and the fire department was called and they ruled it suspicious. We always thought our former neighbor and his business partner set the car on fire. The insurance company waived the deductable and paid the repair bill for the damage to the car. Where we bought the car, a man gave us a pickup truck so we could finish our moving; free of charge. He always had a little crush on mom and so giving her the truck was a big help for us. Our former neighbor caught me at BI-LO grocery store and said "I hope you do take a dead docket because I have plans to have you charged every day or week until you cannot prove your innocence". Before the assault, mom and I went to different meetings and told people and elected officials about the indictment transcript of me being illegal and how it violates the Constitution. We wrote a letter trying to stop the District Attorney Livingstone and the Courts. We met Presidential Candidate George W. Bush and a strong supporter, the highest Marine our friend Gen. Four Star. We met them both in North Avenue, across the river, at Heroes Overlook. We had a sit down with the General Fourstar. He gave us a rude awakening saying "you can't stop them devils from destroying you and doing what they want to do because they have friends and family in powerful positions". He gave us a battle plan to follow, he put pen to paper and put down one; continue to file cases with or without a lawyer, and two; tear down their respect by others and tell your story, even put signs in your yard telling your story. "These people can be torn down by freedom of speech when you follow my game plan and hit them with the truth and with evidence. They will not challenge you as you show the willingness to be forceful with the truth". We told General Fourstar about the District Attorney Livingstone assaulting me and he suggested that we charge him. He said "this man is arrogant of his power and the law". He asked to read the transcript of the indictment and he said "this is a corrupt fool's work that violates the constitution". He told us we will be victorious as long as we follow his war plan. We said "Yes Sir"! Atty. George W. Bush was elected and we filed several appeals and one was a re-trial hearing by the biased Superior Court Judge.

We finally got a court date and Mr. D. was a no-show. The Assistant District Attorney Colby was up there with the judge when my name was called. He suggested that the state would just resolve the case. I and mom waited for the end of the court and we both went up there and said "what did you tell the judge". He said "we don't want to prosecute; we're just going to resolve the case". I said, at the same time mom said "LIKE HELL YOU ARE! you've indicted me, and forced us out of our homes, we ARE going to trial". He spoke up and said "We really don't want to do this". I told the Assistant District Attorney Colby about Jack and what he had said in the store and he said "I don't know anything about that". I said "I will not accept ANY dead dockett; we plan to fully fight the charge".

We went to a community meeting called the Citizens for Good Government. I was talking to a publisher of The Metro Spirit which was a newspaper in the area. While I was talking to him, the District Attorney Livingstone rapped me on the shoulder aggressively saying "I want to talk to you NOW". I went back over to my mom who was sitting at our table with Ms. Intellect and I told them about what happened. Mom said that she was going to call the law and file a police report. I filed a police report and then filed for a warrant for the District Attorney Livingstone. We had to wait about two months for the hearing but the month before that, he came over to mom at that months community meeting and said "Wunderlich is accusing me of assaulting him". Mom told him, "You did". As he was leaving, mom told him "you may win by hook or by crook but you will lose in the end, and if you don't correct this mistake, it will be very costly and highly embarrassing".

We had the hearing for the warrant for the District Attorney Livingstone. I sequestered all the witnesses, so they all had to wait in the hallway. His first witness was one of his good friends... He came into the hearing and testified to the fact that his testimony was only to repay a favor to the District Attorney Livingstone and when I cross-examined him he kept saying "No assault took place and I didn't witness anything by the stage". I corrected him saying "the assault took place by the dessert table". I also asked him "so tell me, what was served for dinner that night"? He said "spaghetti" I said "if you would've been there, you would've known that the dinner that night was barbeque chicken with coleslaw, potato salad and a pot luck of desserts". The witness sat there silently looking at me. The Assistant Magistrate finally looked around and said "I've had enough, Mr. Wunderlich, let's have this witness step down". He proceeded to step down and the next witness, the wife of the president of the Citizens for Good Government, took the stand. When she was being examined by the District Attorney Livingstone's attorney, she said "I did not witness any assault". The District Attorney Livingstone's attorney replied, "Okay, it's your witness now" and he looked to me. I stood up and said to the woman "you said that you did not see an assault take place" she said "that's correct" I said "did I go near the stage that night, where the dignitaries were seated" she said "no, you did not go anywhere near the stage that night" she then asked me "where did the assault take place" I said "by the dessert table" she said "that could be possible, you're a good honest man and you wouldn't lie about anything. The District Attorney Livingstone is a good man also" I said "no further questions and there's no questions pending. This witness can step down" she started to say something else and the Assistant Magistrate said "you may step down, there is no questions, you are free to go". The third witness came in, the brother-in-law. The

District Attorney Livingstone's attorney asked him questions about him charging me. The neighbor's brother-in-law said" Wunderlich is a miserable person, the neighborhood would be better off if he wasn't there" The District Attorney Livingstone's attorney said "no further questions, this witness is yours now" and he looked back at me. I stood up and walked around said "were you at the meeting that night" and he said "no" and I said "are you a member of the Citizens of Good Government committee" he said "no, I've never been one" then I looked around at the District Attorney Livingstone and his attorney and said" do you really want me to question him" they didn't give me a response and I said "okay, let's have at it" I looked at witness and said "well, you don't know anything about the assault, but since you're here then we'll just go ahead and ask you questions about the charges You swore that

you had a gun taken away from me. Where is the gun" he said "I don't know" I said "can the gun be brought into court" he said "I don't know" I said "okay, you said my yard is bugged, have you ever been in my yard" he paused for a long time and finally said "No" I said "okay, you took a petition around and got people to sign it, is that correct" he said "yes" I said "you forged some of the signatures on this petition, is that correct" he paused and he finally said "no I did not do that" I said "that's not true, we have been checking the signatures on the petition and find that the handwriting of the signature directly matches yours and your brother-in-law" he sat there looking at me and didn't say a word. The Assistant Magistrate said "this has gone far enough, I want this witness to step down" he then asked District Attorney Livingstone's lawyer if he had any other witnesses, and he said no. The Assistant Magistrate then turned to me and asked me the same "Mr. Wunderlich, do you have any other witnesses" I said "yes, I do, my mother B. Wunderlich and Ms. Intellect, and myself" I called mom up, asked her some questions, she answered them and the District Attorney Livingstone's attorney said he had no questions. I then called Ms. Intellect, asked her some questions, and she said that what the District Attorney Livingstone did violates ethics rules. I said "thank you, no further questions" I turned to the District Attorney Livingstone's attorney, I said "your witness". He said "no questions". The Assistant Magistrate told Miss Intellect to step down and he said "Mr. Wunderlich, you may take the stand".

The Assistant Magistrate told me "you really don't need to testify, I have heard enough, but if you want to, it's up to you". The Assistant Magistrate looked to the District Attorney Livingstone's attorney "do you have any questions for Mr. Wunderlich" he said "yes". I said "I'm going to go ahead and give my statement; the assault took place that night by the dessert table, not by the stage by one witness testimony". When the D.A's attorney started asking me questions, I answered them and he went over and was whispering to the District Attorney Livingstone. I said to the District Attorney Livingstone's attorney "I have a question to ask you" he said "I don't have to answer your questions". The Assistant Magistrate asked me to ask him the question, instead of directing it to District Attorney Livingstone's attorney, and if he thought it was relevant, he then would ask District Attorney Livingstone's attorney. I said "my question is, since his last name is the same as my lawyer's last name, is he related to my attorney". The Assistant Magistrate then asked District Attorney Livingstone's attorney "I really want to know this answer too". The District Attorney Livingstone's attorney said "no, I am no relation to your attorney". Assistant Magistrate said "that was a very good question Mr. Wunderlich" he looked at District Attorney's attorney and asked if he had any more questions, he said "no" and the Assistant Magistrate said "Mr. Wunderlich, you may step down". I stepped down and went over and sat at my table. The Assistant Magistrate said "I am ready to make a ruling, I cannot give you the warrant for the District Attorney Livingstone at this time but, when the District Attorney Livingstone is no longer in office, Mr. Wunderlich you may come back to the court and I or the judge on the bench will issue you a warrant for the District Attorney Livingstone". The Assistant Magistrate stood up angrily removed his robe and flung it on his arm and said "this is a disgrace and this court stands adjourned". We left the courthouse and that was that. The media could not report any story and the Chronicle reported that I was denied a warrant, not reporting the truth. Mom told me that I would be hung within two weeks.

After the hearing, I wrote the Assistant Magistrate a legal petition requesting that a good friend to the District Attorney Livingstone be charged with perjury. He died before the Assistant Magistrate could consider the perjury charge. Later, the Assistant Magistrate decided he could not charge him because Chief Judge, Superior Court Judge, and the District Attorney Livingstone would not allow the charge.

Within two weeks, like mom said, I got my court date. We went to court and my attorney asked the court to consider dismissing the charges because there could be no corroboration between the witnesses and their statements. They started the jury selections and the woman we evicted was one of the jurors, and she contaminated the jury. She told the jury about us evicting her and later in jury selection, when they asked the jurors if anyone knew me, she stood up. She said that I had evicted her and in no way could she find me not guilty. Mr. D. asked for her to be removed and for a new jury, but Superior Court Judge denied the request. Most of the jury was constructed of county and state employees or spouses of employees, and most of them were connected to state mental hospital employees. The foreperson of my jury served two prior juries and my jury over the past seven months. The jury was selected, and the witnesses were called forward. One of my star witnesses, that could've proved my innocence easily, was Orchard County Deputy Sheriff but he was sent home by the prosecute in lue of threats to lose his job. I lost my star witness and they made mom stay outside the courtroom; she couldn't even testify. There was no evidence or proof on their side, and they would not allow us to show any proof on our side. Jack was the first witness the prosecutor called. He said that the terroristic threats took place in my *back* yard in the afternoon and then he went on to say how impossible it is to live next to me and those we were killing his livelihood. The complainant, the neighbor's brother-in- law, was the next witness, and he claimed that the threat was given in my *front* yard, when he was taking his daughter to school in the morning. When the neighbor's brother-in-law was asked by my attorney if he had signed his daughter in for being late to school he said "no, I didn't". My attorney asked the neighbor's brother-in-law "what did you and your brother-in-law do, reach into a bucket for a day, afternoon time"? Superior Court Judge said "Mr. D., you will stick to asking questions, not making statements". My attorney looked at Superior Court Judge and said "Judge, Jack and his brother-in-law have not corroborated and their written statement and sworn statement shows it, this case should be dismissed". Superior Court Judge said

"Overruled, ask your next question or sit down". My attorney said "no further questions, but Judge, this may be a walk on the gangplank but the state cannot prove their case, this case should be dismissed, there is no proof of a crime being committed". Superior Court Judge said "Overruled, sit down Mr. D.". The prosecutor called investigator Carmel to testify. "Mr. Carmel, have you spoken to Mr. Wunderlich". He said "yes, he's been in our office trying to show us tapes of drug deals and children being raped, I did not watch the video, I finally told Mr. Wunderlich 'you need to leave this office NOW, we will not help you harass your neighbors', Mr. Wunderlich then made a rude comment when leaving, 'damn, you guys must be on their payroll'". "I almost wanted to arrest him there for that comment, but I didn't". The prosecutor then asked "did you advise Mr. Wunderlich never to return to this office again"? Carmel said "yes I did, I informed him that if he came to my office ever again then I would arrest him. LT. DET. Bee also told Mr. Wunderlich 'you either do what they are doing or move, when in Rome, do what the Romans do' and this upset Mr. Wunderlich and his mother stated to my friend that he was a disgrace to the badge. Mr. Wunderlich started writing letters accusing our office of taking sides". The prosecutor asked if that was true. Mr. Carmel said no. The prosecutor said "what do you think about Mr. Wunderlich charging our boss, the District Attorney Livingstone". Mr. Carmel said "Mr. Wunderlich must be a real mental case to go after his neighbors and District Attorney Livingstone with unproven allegations and charges. I hope after this trial Mr. Wunderlich will get some mental help". "Mr. D., your witness" Superior Court Judge barked at Mr. D. "Mr. D., you will only ask questions, not makes statements". My attorney said "okay Judge, Investigator Carmel, did

Jack or his brother-in-law has any proof of a crime being committed". Carmel said no. "Investigator Carmel, can *you* prove of a crime being committed"? Carmel said no. Mr. D. looked at the Judge "Judge, I have to ask the court, we haven't heard anything to prove that a crime was committed, this case should be dismissed". Superior Court Judge said "No, I will not dismiss this case, if you continue to request a dismissal, I will find you in contempt of this court, and do you understand. Ask your next question or sit down". Mr. D. said "no more questions Judge". Superior Court Judge turned to the prosecutor, "do you have any more witnesses"? The prosecutor had a blank look on his face "I don't know Your Honor". The prosecutor turned to his team of six prosecutors and then back to the Judge "No more witnesses". Superior Court Judge turned to my attorney "Do you have any more witnesses Mr. D." He said "yes, I have some witnesses but the court and the prosecutor sent my star witness home". Superior Court Judge asked "who". Mr. D. replied "Deputy Sheriff". Superior Court Judge said "yes, he won't testify against his county and state; pick your next witnesses". If Deputy Sheriff would've testified, he would have told the court that he was at my residence that day in the morning and afternoon, and that no threats were given in his presence. He was there in the morning around 9:30 following a call from the neighbor's brother- in-law saying that I was issuing threats, and he was also there in the early afternoon pertaining to a gun war that was happening at Jack's house. These were both the times that Jack and his brother-in-law had claimed that the threats were issued. Mr. D. said "I have Wunderlich and his mother". Superior Court Judge said "Yes, Mr. Wunderlich can be allowed to testify, but not his mother". Mr. D. said "Please you're Honor, allows his mother to testify". Superior

Court Judge said "No, she isn't allowed in my courtroom". Mr. D. said "how about allowing us to present evidence"? Superior Court Judge said "again, NO". Mr. D. asked the Judge if he would allow the people who signed the petition to come to the court. Superior Court Judge said no once again. Mr. D. said "what about a letter from our friend Congressman Charles and Our friend Senator Paul (our friend Senator Paul past away the next morning)". Superior Court Judge said no. Mr. D. said "okay Judge, I guess I will call my only witness, R. Wunderlich", and for once, Superior Court Judge said "*yes,* Mr. Wunderlich, you can only answer the questions and you may not bring up any evidence or letters, furthermore, if you try to bring up anything I have told you not to bring up then I will warn you only once and then I will find you in contempt". Superior Court Judge looked like the Devil saying "*Do you understand*"? I said "yes, let's get this <u>thing</u> started". Mr. D. kept asking me leading questions and Superior Court Judge kept objecting, asking like, "Tell us how this started and did you threaten these people". I said no and Superior Court Judge kept objecting. I spoke up to Superior Court Judge saying "Judge, they were making threats to myself and my mother". Superior Court Judge said "I warned you Mr. Wunderlich, you need to sit there and be quiet". Mr. D. said "no more questions at this time". The Judge turned to the prosecutor "you may question Mr. Wunderlich". The prosecutor stood up and turned to me "Wunderlich, you accused the county and state with aiding and abetting your neighbors". I said yes. "Mr. Wunderlich, you have accused our District Attorney Livingstone with assault". I said "yes, I also won that hearing Mr. Prosecutor". The prosecutor said "I don't know who won". I replied "I charged him and have a court order for a warrant for the District Attorney Livingstone when he is no longer in power". The prosecutor said "no further questions". Superior Court Judge turned to my attorney "do you have any questions for Mr. Wunderlich". Mr. D. said "yes Judge". Mr. D. turned to me "when was this hearing". I said "about two weeks ago". He said "have you ever spoken to the complainant the neighbor's brother-in-law". I said no. He looked at me questioningly "*No*"? I said, with a hand to heaven, "no". Superior Court Judge said "I'm ready to charge the jury, reasonable doubt is the law", and then he sent the jury into their chambers. The foreperson requested a word with the Judge, stating that she had confused my case with the other two past cases against two other defendants. The Judge quickly corrected her. She said "oh, okay, no evidence in this case". Superior Court Judge said "that's true". She then said "reasonable doubt or probable cause"? Superior Court Judge said "probable cause will be sufficient in this case". That's when I KNEW I was screwed. The Judge changed the rules of the court to get me convicted. The jury came back in 45 minutes, and they found me Guilty. Mr. D. quickly asked to poll the jury. They all said guilty. I will never forget what happened. The Judge thanked the jury saying "you have done a great service to your community, you are excused". Superior Court Judge then ordered the bailiff to take me into custody. I exited, crying and telling my mother not to worry about this. She said "I love you Wunderlich".

I was taken to jail and then Superior Court Judge ordered me to return to the courtroom, so he could abuse me even further. He demanded that I admit to committing the crime I was convicted. "You need to admit you did the crime". I said "I am innocent; I refuse to admit that I committed any crime". Superior Court Judge said "I will pass punishment after you have a full mental evaluation;

I want to know what makes you tick". He then asked what I thought about the trial. I said "this was a hanging, may God have mercy on everyone". He said "Take him to jail, now". I arrived back at the jail and was confined for 45 days again. I was sent to the State Mental Hospital. A female guard was going to shackle my ankles but she knew my mother, so she had mercy on me. Another officer showed up, a superior officer, and got mad at her for not shackling me. I spoke up and said "they will cut me sergeant, please don't put them on me, I already have problems and I promised my mother I wouldn't do anything to make it worse for her". He reluctantly said "I believe you, so we will trust you not to escape".

I said "You have my word sergeant". I was taken into custody by the hospital. Two days later a fellow inmate escaped and the guard looked at me and I said "go and get him, I will sit right here". The guard said it was okay. Later he said he believed I wouldn't run away and I said "my situation is bad, there's no sense in making it worse". My mother came to visit me every day. Unfortunately the Judge found out, and he ordered me back to jail.

While I was at the mental hospital, I made the best out of a very bad situation. I met a very huge guy that was deathly afraid of thunder. One night we had a storm come in and he was sitting next to me on the sofa. The nurses and orderlies came into the room trying to get this big man off the sofa to tie him down before the storms thunder rolls in. I had told the guy that thunder was the angels and God bowling, and we are safe inside the building, besides he was a pretty big guy. The nurses came over to me and said "Wow! Mr. Wunderlich, you calmed the giant, we couldn't do that, and he wouldn't listen to us". I said "I studied sociology and psychology in school so talking to someone on their level comes easy to me". My mother would come see me every day and I would call her every day and night. I was always relieved when she answered the phone because the threats on Jack and his friends. One night another patient was caught in the bathroom doing something wrong and an orderly confronted him and the patient accused him of a crime and I was in the shower and witnessed the whole thing. I was a witness for the orderly. The patient's family ended up moving him to another mental facility and the orderly still worked at the hospital. The orderly was always thankful to me for my statement. The hospital kept trying to get me to sign papers. I finally refused to sign any papers after advice from my lawyer and my mom. My birthday was coming up and my mom asked me what I wanted and I said Chinese food so she brought me my birthday lunch. The doctors and staff proceeded to bring me into a room and diagnosed me with and illness and ordered me to take medicine. I thought this was wrong because they had only talked to me for 5 minutes in 3 sessions. We always had interruptions from other patients fighting and coming into the room. Mom always brought me money for store calls. The hospital told me if I didn't sign the papers then they were going to send me back to jail. I said bye. When I was getting up to leave I looked at the doctor and started to say "how can you diagnose me when we haven't had more than five minutes to talk. Doctor we haven't met at all". I accused them of misdiagnosing me and the doctor having a nose in the air sickness because of on many occasions I said good morning and or good afternoon and sometimes goodnight. He felt that he was better than everyone including the coworkers. He ignores them too. I suggested "could I meet your doctors, doctor, because I think you're nuts also, maybe your doctor would give me a better and more true diagnoses". He spoke up and said "we are done here". I suggested "why don't you ask my mother to come in here and give her diagnoses just like the one you gave me. Maybe I could watch when she hits you or tells you off". He said "you are free to go". I said "you sir are a quack and I refuse to sign the diagnoses form". He stormed out of the room. A few days later I was taken back to jail to wait for sentencing. I was picked to be the new houseman of our cell block. I did store call, take and hand out laundry, clean the bathrooms, showers and the dining areas. If anything wasn't clean, our visitation would be cut on visitation day. I was still the checkers champion. I could count all my losses on one hand. No one could beat me, not even the officers on duty. They also gave me the job handing out linen to all the new inmates. The other inmates bought me store call to say thanks for being an awesome houseman and I asked them to make my assistant the new houseman. He declined it because there was too much responsibility and problems.

On my sentencing day, I was taken to court. Before going, I gave my chips, candy bars, and sodas to my assistant house man because other inmates and deputies would go into any inmates room looking to see what they could steal before going to court. Once at the courthouse, I was put in a holding cell waiting for my turn. My attorney's partner was asked to take over the case. He knew Superior Court Judge disliked him and he left to go to Texas. His partner, Mr. Pitts, told the Judge he drove Mr. D. to the airport. I was asked if Mr. Pitts was okay with me to handle my case. I finally got my chance to be sentenced. Superior Court Judge proved his nick-name was true; Stick It Superior Court Judge. He said "Mr. Wunderlich, I want you to admit to this crime". I said "NO, No, Never, I did not threaten anyone at any time". My lawyer spoke up and said "Your Honor there is no evidence that a crime was actually committed". The Judge looked at the prosecutor and the prosecutor called my lawyer over so he could have a word with him. Mr. Pitts came back over to where me and my mother were sitting and he asked me "have you ever worked a day in your life". I said "yes, I worked at hotels, motels, restaurants, convenience stores, I was a demonstrator of products in grocery stores and I also delivered newspapers with my mom". He then asked me if I went to church. I said "yes, I was baptized two months ago at Victory Baptist Church in North Avenue". He asked if I was Baptist. I said "my father was Catholic and my mom is Christian, so naturally I went to Christian churches. What's going on, why is the court interested in my work habit and my religion". He said "the Judge is trying to give you the maximum sentence, five years in prison instead of probation, I am trying my best to get you probation". Mom told my attorney "this case was a circus and we will fight it". On the Thursday when I was sentenced, Superior Court Judge gave me five years intensive probation where I could not write or send letters to any elected officials. He said "thank God I will not get any more letters from you; I got more letters from you than I got from my family the whole time I was in the military. Mr. Wunderlich, if I get anymore letters from you then I will give you five years in prison and if anyone tells me that they are getting letters from you, I will also give you five years". He ordered me an eight pm curfew and ordered me to be on the medication I was prescribed from the hospital. It was only one milligram of respidal. "Mr. Wunderlich, you are making a big deal over 1 milligram" Superior Court Judge said, scrutinizing. He said "And if you refuse to take this medication or follow the other conditions of this probation, I will order you five years in prison".

He also ordered that no knives or weapons will be in the house and that the house was subject to searches. They never did search the house. I was taken out of the courtroom to go back to jail to wait my release. My attorney told my mother that she could go and pick me up after I was released. Chief Probation officer Maxwell, the head of the probation office, told my mom to have me contact his office tomorrow. Mom said "tomorrow is a holiday; this is a four day holiday weekend". He said "okay, we will contact him". Tuesday and Wednesday came and went, and there was no contact.

Chief Probation officer Maxwell and the checkup probation officer called me acting very hostile. I quickly responded telling Chief Probation officer Maxwell that mom told him we would be getting a call from him because of the four day weekend. They quickly apologized and said "you need to report to us today for intake". I went to intake and spent an hour in the lobby waiting for the checkup probation officer. He finally came out and I apologized for the miscommunication and he apologized too saying "this is a rare occasion, we don't ever apologize to a probationer. He was taking me back to his office and Chief Probation officer Maxwell came walking his probationer out and apologizing to me. His probationer said "damn, that is unreal that never happens". When I was in his office I met probation officer and another man. "They will be supervising you; they will be conducting a house search. Searching for guns, knives, and other contraband". The checkup probation officer asked me if I had anything to say. I said "yes, my mother is very old and all I ask is that nobody from this office will put handcuffs on her and lay her on the ground". The checkup probation officer said "We have a job to do and that is what we do". I responded "if anyone hurts her then she will charge them okay, after all, you gave me over four days, I could have moved the trailer across the state".

Poor checkup probation officer, he kept following us and mom, being a former law enforcement officer, kept losing him. We made fun of losing him often. I won that part and nobody came to the house to search it. Mr. Probation officer was a very good and honest young guy. He kept saying "after reviewing the trial transcripts, how did they get a conviction and intensive probation Mom said "by corruption". I didn't have to pay any fine of fees because I hired a new lawyer, Atty. Lucas Law. When I had to report in, all was good, even though I felt like a POW at the time, I went in once a month. One day the checkup probation officer called me into his office and said "the judge has ordered you to the state mental hospital to get re-examined". I said okay. I went, but after going to my re-trial with Atty. Lucas Law and Superior Court Judge. The District Attorney Livingstone threatened my attorney and any other attorney could not defend me. My mom told Atty. Lucas Law, "Please come to us if you get any threats". He promised. He also went to federal court and filed a petition to the Chief Jude of Federal Court and Assistant Judge of Federal Court of the U.S. District Court. They gave me the legal powers of pro-se and District Attorney Livingstone asked the federal judges what my powers are and he was told "you will treat him as one of our attorneys and not yours District Attorney Livingstone", because their District Attorney Livingstone had almost assaulted one of his assistant District Attorney Mr. Peeks. I went to the hospital and met an honest doctor; he was a good man and looked like Burl Ives on The Christmas Story. He reviewed my files and said the medication was all wrong for me and the illness was wrong too. He said he was going to give me a new illness and a new medication. Then, before saying he questioned me, I said "wait a minute before you give me that illness, let me go get some papers from the car". He said "okay, please come back to my office". So I went back to his office with the papers and he asked a question, but I knew if I started talking then he would think I was nuts, so I suggested getting the papers for him. He started reading the papers and asking me questions and I answered his questions. When he got to the last page of the papers and he said "what is this" and I said "what page are you on". He said "it's something about giving you federal powers of pro-se". I said "Awesome, how fast can you get me my files under the freedom of information act". He said "okay, I will give you a copy of your files". I had threatened to go to federal court to get an order; he said "that's not necessary". I said "before you sign on giving me another illness and medications I have a second opinion outside of the state and when I return I will charge you with appeasing the corrupt Judge and District Attorney Livingstone". He spoke up and said "No, I won't do that, you are free to go"

The doctor gave me one page of my hospital record that indicated that I could take medication at my own discretion. I called the checkup probation officer and said "we need to meet ASAP!" He said "come NOW". I said okay and I stopped and made copies. When I walked into his office I said "I am here as pro-se, not probationer". He said okay. I said "here, I want you to tell the Judge and the District Attorney Livingstone to take the medicine and the hospital and shove it up their ASSES!" I also showed him how they had influenced the mental evaluation. He said "how did you get this", I said "I used my federal powers to get all copies of my files". As I was leaving, I turned around and asked for an extension of my curfew to go to the Republican Gala. "We are the guest of our friend

Congressman Charles". He said "okay, have fun Mr. Wunderlich". I said "writing letters is prohibited right"? He said "right". I said "not if I ask them to write me so I can write them". He said "that voids the order Mr. Wunderlich".

Mr. Probation officer followed us or better yet, tried to follow us every so often. Mom would spot him and lose him every time. We would go on signing with Ms. Intellect and Mom would drive us. I would witness the signings and Miss Intellect was the notary. Miss Intellect knew money was tight for us so she would pay me 25 to 35 dollars and put gas in the car. We also work for campaigns for the Republican cause and they would pay for our gas. I worked at some stores taking out the trash so I could get cans to recycle and also find winning lottery tickets that had been thrown away. Life was hard, but we made it with God's help. Mom was and is the master of making cheap dinners tastes AWESOME! Thank God for Ms. Intellect and her father David, they always got us tickets to campaign dinners and parties. The Sherriff died and Chief became our new sheriff. He apologized at Major Superstore for giving those drug dealers, child pimps, and car choppers the charge against me. We told him and the Republican Party we are going to clean house, they always laughed at us. When the Judge and the District Attorney Livingstone lost more probation conditions against me, they got a lying corrupt officer to stop my mother for speeding, and we were between two cars. Mom had to go to court and that's when we learned not to talk to the prosecutor. They act so cordial and pretend to be your friend. While we were waiting for our name to be called, people in and outside the courtroom started whispering "we have a Wunderlich in the courtroom..." this made me laugh. I looked at a woman beside us and introduced myself. "I am R. Wunderlich" and I offered her my hand. She was shocked, but shook my hand. My mother was telling people downstairs how corrupt the law is and how I was inside the courtroom being treated like a dignitary by the people. When we finally got called, mom was suffering from a vocal cord problem and we offered our tape we had made of the illegal stopping of us. The judge had already heard of our tape and refused to hear it. Also, the prosecutor, after speaking with us, used everything we were going to use. The judge was Judge Lefty, a law judge that always ruled on the side of the law. He passed judgment, 50 dollars fine; 15 dollars court cost, for a total of $65. We went up to pay it and that pissed off the prosecutor who was standing behind us.

On September 11, 2001, the checkup probation officer said I had to come down and pay my first probation fee and fine to the office. I named it the "mafia protection" and they hated me for calling it that. I had pushed the wheelchair up to the bar and I couldn't move with the prosecutor standing behind me. I saw the judge getting irritated and so I slammed my hand on his side bar and said "Judge Lefty, if you don't move this guy from behind me then I will charge him with false imprisonment and kidnapping", he said "under whose authority".

I spoke up and said "I have the power of pro-se the U.S. District Court, the Chief Judge of Federal Court and Assistant Judge of Federal Court". He spoke up to the prosecutor and said "what and why are you standing there for". The prosecutor said that he wanted to talk to me. The Judge said "Go sit down NOW". As I was leaving he stood up to show defiance and Judge Lefty spoke up again "I said sit down NOW!" I said "that's a good puppy dog, do as you are told". We left the courtroom laughing at the prosecutor and the judge had to restore order to the courtroom. In 2002, we helped the Republicans gain power of the state for the first time in 135 plus years. Sherriff told his deputies at every meeting to leave us alone and treat us with respect. Some lap-dogs for their District Attorney Livingstone, Chief Judge, Superior Court Judge, and the late Sherriff continued to harass us by shining their lights in our house, pulling us over, and taunting us.

In 2003, I and my mom were switching back and forth filing cases. The last case mom filed, the state wanted to sanction and arrest her. Mom filed back and said "Hell, you cost me everything we owned and stole money from us. All I have left is me, come and get me". The Chief Judge of Federal Court and Assistant Judge of Federal Court were considering having her picked up, but after reading my filing I said "wait a minute, we have been hurt enough so that's how I got the filing power of pro-se". They ordered me to file a habeas corpus in the State Superior Court.

In 2004, I was told by Commissioner Rose to request going to the commissioners and air my problems to the mayor and the commissioners for 5 minutes. So I did and I believe it made a difference in my punishment. My probation officer started giving me extensions in curfew, but one day he called me into his office to tell me that I will have to notify him before going to the state capitol Supreme Court. I said "okay". He said "you are free to go". I stepped out of his office and then stepped back in and said "sit down". He said "this meetings over". I said "with the probationer, yes, now with the pro-se, as the pro-se, I don't have to tell you anything pertaining to my case". The checkup probation officer said he was under orders to stop me from filing any more cases in any more courts. I said "I fully intend to fight this bullshit and I refuse to report what I'm doing to the judge's secretary". One early morning Mom woke me up to file a case. I said "I better call my probation officer". Mom said "no, we are not calling the Judge, and by calling my probation officer you're calling the Judge". We left that morning and picked up a female tail, and it was so obvious that mom said "don't look now; we have a stupid deputy following us". We were heading to a neighboring county and mom got into the right lane. Then when the car was coming behind us to exit, mom moved over to the left lane, which kept the woman from tailing us any further. She had no choice, she went right and we went left. By the time she was able to turn around, we were hiding behind some bushes at Racetrack Convenience Store and she had lost us. We had breakfast and started heading to the state capitol. Just 15 minutes outside the state capitol, Mom had me call the checkup probation officer.

I filed my case, telling the do nothing State Supreme Court about Chief Judge and the District Attorney Livingstone forcing us out of our homes. This was another waste of time and money because this God awful place sticks up for family, friends, and inbreaders. We came back to the city and I hit my 1st carwash and found a suspicious package addressed to any female soldier. I cleared the carwash to one side and moved the box to the safest side, away from the gas pumps. The law and bomb squad showed up finally, along with a bomb dog, and the fire dept. The fire department Chief jumped all over me for moving the box. I remembered Spock on Startrek, the one of many outnumber the needs of many. I stood my ground and said I believed I did the right thing. Just that moment, the bomb dog sat down right next to the box and looked up at his handler. The officer said "everyone needs to leave, RIGHT NOW". I never found out what was inside the box. I went and called the checkup probation officer from the 1st store I had worked for and he said "I already know you are a hero, I have an order to pick you up. You filed a charge you have no proof for". I asked what and he said "Superior Court Judge wants you in jail". I said "I can prove it; it's in the habeas corpus hearing transcript". He said he had to go; he was going to talk to the judge about my proof. I said "you blurted it out about 'they forced you to move, not me' and I asked him 'whose they' and he said 'Chief Judge and District Attorney Livingstone so I filed the case, and in 2004, I went to the Mayor and commissioners to tell them about the corruption of the law, the judicial system, and the District Attorney Livingstone". We hung up the phones and I went on cleaning my gas stations and convenience stores. I would clean the stores; stock the coolers, clean the restrooms and take trash out, and sweep the parking lot. Everyday was the same routine. We would leave the house at 11 am and get back around 8 pm with just a few minutes to spare. We would look for lottery tickets and recycle cans, copper, brass, and hard aluminum. We were driving a Ford Escort car we had bought from a title pawn friend for 900 dollars. Rich, one of the managers of the convenience store, was doing remodeling on the store and told me I could have whatever I could carry. It took us nearly seven hours to put all the metal in that little car. The next day I went to the gas station and Rich said "you couldn't have put all that into that car". He came out and asked mom and she said "thank you, and yes we did".

Chief Probation officer Maxwell was very big now at the probation office. He came out to get me. He knew my mother from a hotel she worked at. He would leave her names, pictures of wanted probationers, and she would call him. He asked me if I wanted anything, I said extensions in curfew; and I got it.

We took the cans and metal to recycle. It took four trips and we made 150 dollars considering my mafia protection and fine, we had 60 dollars to the good. The other stores that knew me knew I was honest and very dependable. I wouldn't do anything to hurt my stores or employees. Ms. Danzell gave two guys permission to sleep behind the store. She worked for the same company as Rich. One day I went to the store and overheard one guy and an employee for Mr. PAYROLL asking questions like when do they open, close, and how many employees usually closed. I thought that was strange. That night I was watching the news and they were describing two men that had escaped from a prison work detail. The one that stuck to me was the one with the spider web tattoo on his forehead. I called the store and informed Ms. Ms. Roarke about the two guys behind the store. She said thank you. The manager Danzell lost her promotion to general manager because they found out how she gave two guys permission to camp behind the store. Not from me. She told me my services were no longer needed and I said okay and goodbye. Ms. Hazel was the manager of Mr. PAYROLL and she gave me a free stack of check cashing coupons so we could get our checks cashed for free.

I always went to the probation office, not as the probationer but every now and then as pro-se. Every time I filed a case, I would bring the checkup probation officer a copy of what I filed. This way he would have some heads up. I filed a case in U.S. District Court one day and me, the checkup probation officer, and Mr. Poze got into an argument in the lobby about me filing cases against county, state, and his office. We got so loud that Mr. Jerry couldn't do his intake of a probationer. He came into the lobby and said "excuse me, I can't hear my intake", then he turned to me, "are you a probationer"? I said "yes, but not today, I'm pro-se". He looked at me and said "what's pro-se" and I looked at him and said "damn, you work in the law and don't know what pro-se means"? He looked at the checkup probation officer and said "You and Poze, what is going on here. We need to have a meeting". They both said no. I said "Mr. Jerry, pro-se means I can represent myself". He said "okay, how does he have legal powers my probation officer". The checkup probation officer said "Two judges in the U.S. District Court have given him legal powers equal to a U.S. Attorney". Jerry said "my probation officer when I get done with my intake we need to talk; Mr. Wunderlich, why are you arguing with the checkup probation officer and Poze". I said, "I am innocent and was hung by the corrupt District Attorney Livingstone, Superior Court Judge, Chief Judge, and Law". He said "you may leave", and so I left. Later that night I had my probation officer come over to the house and tell us that their Chief, Franklin had come from the state capitol to find out what was going on here. Mom said good, because my probation officer had driven down the dirt mud hole before getting to our house and every time he would ask us, "Who owns this mud hole". Mom would say "we do, why, I wanted the state to pave it to save my cars paint job". I went and put cat litter and bagged concrete into the mud hole, and he hit it, and said "who put that concrete here" and I said "I have no idea". One day someone switched water covers with us and the water department turned our water off by mistake. We called the water department and they insisted on me to turn the water back on. I said "I'm not touching it, you better get out here and turn my water back on". This old man was driving down our dirt road acting pissed. He hit the concrete and said "HOT DAMN!!!". We could hear him from our trailer. We had a hard time keeping a straight face from laughing. He said "did you know someone put concrete in your mud hole". I looked at him, trying to keep a straight face, and said "They Did"?

We moved and started preparing for the habeas corpus hearing.

Mom served a subpoena to Mayor Goodman at a republican breakfast. We got the court date and we went to court, the first habeas corpus hearing 130 years. I was pushing mom in her wheelchair when we arrived at the hearing. Atty. Lucas Law was standing at the hearing room door beside the number one state attorney. He asked "Atty. Lucas Law, are the Wunderlich's here yet". Atty. Lucas Law said "yes, they just arrived, that's the Wunderlich's right there", me and mom were passing by. While we were waiting, Atty. Lucas Law was talking with my probationer. The bailiff came to the door and said "Wunderlich's, please come into the room". We entered and the room was completely packed. People were sitting and standing all around, and Chief Judge was sitting atop the bench, looking like an arrogant fool. Chief Judge was trying to clear out the room and I tried to help him and asked if I could sequester all of the witnesses. Chief Judge responded by saying, "yes, that's a good idea". He gave an order for all of the witnesses to rise and exit the courtroom, into the hallway, but to stay there so that they could hear their name being called. Chief Judge said "bailiff, please come help Mrs. Wunderlich with her chair and move her into the hallway". At that same time, the state attorney made my probation officer go into the hallway also. I said "wait a minute Judge, she isn't a witness, so she can remain in the courtroom". Chief Judge said "is she representing you"? I said "no, she's my moral support". Chief Judge, after deliberation, finally said "okay, she can stay". A woman, wearing a press badge, walked into the courtroom. She walked along the isles and saw that all the seats were taken. Chief Judge said "you will have to leave". I looked at mom, and I had my tote sitting in a seat behind me, and I said "wait a minute, Your Honor, I will remove my bag for the lady to sit". Chief Judge gave me a stern look. I said "Judge, let's get this hearing underway, I am eager to win my freedom". Chief Judge said "okay Mr. Wunderlich, call you first witness". I called Mayor Goodman, who was in a hurry because he had a meeting to attend after he left. I looked at Mayor Goodman and said, "Mayor Goodman, have you ever spoken to me, or to my neighbor's brother-in-law about me "? He declared "no, I have never spoken ill of you to anyone". After a few more questions, he was dismissed and he said "Thank you mother and Wunderlich for calling me first, I'll see you later, and good luck", then he left. The next witness I had subpoenaed, District Attorney Livingstone, had not appeared, and he didn't even use his executive privilege. The next witness I called was the neighbor's brother-in-law. I told Chief Judge "I wish to treat the witness as a hostile witness. The state attorney said "you can't do that, he is the states complainant". I said, "I subpoenaed him, did you"? He said no. Chief Judge said "he is a witness at this time". The neighbor's brother-in-law was very nervous and I started asking him questions once he was sworn in. "Have you ever spoken to me before today". He said "yes, in a hearing against their District Attorney Livingstone and before". I said "what time was it, AM or PM"? He said "both". I said "you swore you spoke to the Mayor, right"? He said "yes, about you harassing me". I said "when did you speak to the Mayor"? He said "a week before charging you". I said "that's not true, you never spoke to the mayor, in fact, and the mayor denies ever speaking to you". Chief Judge said "Mr. Wunderlich, you cannot put one witness against another". I said "Judge, you heard Mayor Goodman clearly say that he had not spoken to the witness about me, period". Chief Judge said "carry on". I said "you never spoke to the mayor, and I know that for a fact because he wasn't in town for two weeks, I was on his campaign. You have lied about me and the Mayor". The witness looked at Chief Judge and addresses the court. "They made you move out, not me" he said. I said "In fact, everything you said is a lie, you even lied about the gun, you also said the yard was bugged, have you ever been in my yard". I padded some tapes and said "I believe I can prove you've been in my yard". He finally admitted "yes, one time". I said "But that's a lie also, I have three tapes proving different days you entered my yard". He said "yes, I have been in your yard". I asked, "Did you find any bugs or listening devices"? He said "No". I moved that the neighbor's brother-in-law should remain in the hallway and that made him angry so he stood up and started acting threateningly to me. A F.B.I. agent sitting behind me said that if something wasn't done to contain the hostile witness, then he would have to take action to protect Mom and I. Chief Judge said "Yes, you may remain in the hallway and you may call your next witness Mr. Wunderlich". I called Jack. He came up and was sworn in. I said "Jack, you are under oath, I can prove you were the one making threats". He said no. I said, padding the tapes, "I can prove it". Jack said "I was the one making threats". Chief Judge came unglued "wait a minute, did I just wake up, do you know what you just admitted to me"? Jack said "yes, I do". Chief Judge said "you just admitted to me and this court that you were making threats to Mr. Wunderlich". He said "Yes, I have made threats because they have ruined my business". The state attorney spoke up and said "Judge I have been holding off my objections to this hearing because this hearing appears to be a retrial hearing instead of a habeas corpus hearing". I feel this was just a tactic to stop Jack from being charged from making threats. Chief Judge said "Mr. Wunderlich, what do you say about that"? I said "I have a court order signed by two Honorable Judges in the U.S. District Court to file a habeas corpus case in superior court". He asked to see the order. I handed the order to the state attorney and he looked over it and he handed it to the Clerk of the Court. She looked at it and held it for a minute. Chief Judge exclaimed "What are you doing!!"? She said "I haven't ever seen an order from the federal court before". Chief Judge said "me either, I want to see it". He looked over the order and said "It does look like a court order to file a habeas corpus so I have no choice, let's continue with this hearing, Objection Overruled the state attorney". He had no questions for Jack or his brother-in-law. Chief Judge said "call your next witness Mr. Wunderlich". I called RCSD Deputy Sheriff. He came into the hearing room. I asked "you were at my house in the AM and the PM when the neighbor's brother-in-law called you in the AM". He said yes. "Then in the PM Deputy Sheriff" He said "yes, when you called Mr. Wunderlich". I said "did you witness any threats between me or the neighbor's brother-in-law"? He said "no I did not". I asked "why didn't you testify at my hanging or trial"? He said "the Assistant District Attorney told me to leave NOW". I said "how did that make you feel Deputy Sheriff". He said "I am very sorry for not being allowed to testify at your trial". I said "thank you, no more questions". Chief Judge said "your next witness"? I called for the Assistant District Attorney "You told the hospital that I wasn't any danger to myself or others, is that correct"? He said "no, I don't recall". I said "let me remind you, here's the hospital report". He said "well... yes I did". I said "It was two weeks after my trial, is that correct"? He said "yes". I said "No more questions". The state said "no questions". Chief Judge called the next witness. I said "my former lawyer Attorney. Mr. D.". I said "Mr. D., why were no witnesses or evidence presented at my trial for the defense". He said "the court and the District Attorney 'handcuffed' me on what I could present". I then called Investigator Fallow to the stand. Chief Judge said "okay, let's get started". I asked Investigator Fallow "Sergeant Investigator Fallow..." he said "wait a minute, I was promoted from sergeant". I said "after what you did to me, you got promoted"? I said "what is your title now"? He said "Special Agent in Charge". I said "is it true that you use the word interview instead of interrogation"? He said yes. I said "no Miranda warning was given right"? He said yes. All of a sudden, Chief Judge said "how long have you been an officer Investigator Fallow"? He said "Your Honor, I have for 20 years". Chief Judge said "and now you're an officer in charge of what, so you were given a promotion after the case"? Investigator Fallow said yes. I said "Judge, I have a tape of this interview or interrogation". Chief Judge said "we don't need to listen to it; we have the horse's mouth right here". In my opinion, I think the Judge used the wrong end of the horse. I said "Investigator Fallow, you are free to go". Chief Judge asked the state attorney if he had any witnesses. He said "yes, I have two". He called Atty. Lucas Law to the stand. As he entered, Atty. Lucas Law patted us on the back, greeting us. The state attorney looked in awe. "Atty. Lucas Law, were you paid" the state attorney asked. Atty. Lucas Law said "yes, me and Mr. Wunderlich are in good standings". The state attorney said "no more questions". Chief Judge said "your witness".

I looked at Atty. Lucas Law and asked "were you threatened by the court or District Attorney Livingstone if you filed anything else on my behalf"? He said "yes I was, I was told that if I filed anything for you or any other lawyer does then we could all be charged abusive litigation". The Judge told the state attorney to call his next witness. The state attorney said "I would your honor, but I think Mr. Wunderlich has had enough help for today and I'm not sure what my witness would say". Chief Judge said "who is it". The state attorney said "my probation officer, Mr. Wunderlich's probation officer". Chief Judge asked me, "Do you have any other witnesses to call". I said "Well I do have some questions for *you* but I guess I'll wait until I get into a higher court". Chief Judge and I went back and forth and he said that he would make a ruling at a later date. I said "Judge, to punish me any further, to do so is a violation of my Constitutional rights as an American, I insist on being released right now". Chief Judge said "I can't do that right now". We left the hearing room with the officers and agents help. The hearing lasted 2 hours and 15 minutes.

We started trying to end the probation by filing in a different court and the judge in a neighboring county decided to go fishing instead of making a ruling. The Friday before Monday I called his secretary and left him a message telling him he's a disgrace of the bench and the law profession and that I hoped the hand of God would strike him down. Tuesday we went to the Good Government meeting and Former Speaker of the House, a life-long friend and Democrat who served 30 plus years as Speaker of the House, tried to help us before all the charges were filed against me. We asked him to stop trying to help us to save his legacy as an Elder Statesman. He came over, shook my hand and gave me a hug, and said "Wunderlich needs to run for Mayor". I was surprised that he would say that and I said "why". He said "Wunderlich, you are a very honest decent young man and you were wrongfully charged and convicted. Now you have the respect of the county and state". I went to the funeral home last Thursday to sign President Ronald Reagans Memorial Book. With mom's permission, I signed my true identity saying "the first Just Say No Kid says goodbye to President Ronald Reagan". WoW! They sure moved fast after a man and woman asked what I was signing. The book was turned over to the F.B.I. They took the book and flew it to First Lady Nancy Reagan. At first, her secret service would not allow the two F.B.I. agents entry to the First Lady. The secret service asked her if she wanted to meet the agents and at first she said no, but when one of the agents said that it involves the true identity of the 1st Just Say No Kid, she said "what's his name", the agent said "Wunderlich". She said "that's right, please bring them in". They came in and asked her if it was true. She said "yes, thanks for coming". The two agents left to speak to my Uncle God's toy. He told them the District Attorney Livingstone had harassed him and other family members. That's when some of my family started trying to contact me. They left the meeting with my uncle and when they were flying back they called Chief Judge to have a meeting with him and the District Attorney Livingstone. When they arrived, Chief Judge, Superior Court Judge, and District Attorney spoke with the Clerk of Court, and told her they were having a "closed door" meeting. The agents asked to enter the meeting and at first they refused to answer the door. The agents said "If you don't answer the door we will remove it with a ram door opener". They finally opened the door and the two agents pointed at the county and state powers to be and said "we now know who you hung". Chief Judge said "we haven't hung anyone". One of the agents said "you hung Wunderlich, the first Just Say No Kid, knowing he was an innocent man". Chief Judge said "I quit! I'm not falling dead at his feet in a courtroom".

The same week Former Speaker of the House asked me to run for Mayor, Congresswoman Banker asked me to run for Congress when she caught me making a trip to the state capitol trying to help register our friend Ms. Intellect to run as a Republican. She didn't believe she needed a money order and so the race was on. I headed across the street to the post office and then back to Ms. Intellect. I didn't know that it had become known that I was the first Just Say No Kid. Congresswoman Banks asked me to walk with her to the Democratic part of the government building to talk me into registering and qualifying me to run for Congress as a Democrat. She said "I know we can work together, you will run against Congressman Hampster and Professor Singe". I said "no", I shook their hands and left the chambers. I turned to Ms. Banks and said "thank you but I'm a republican now". She said "okay my dear friend; please send your mother my love". I said okay and hugged and kissed her on the cheek. I left and returned to Ms. Intellect, all the while the Republicans were telling me to run for *any* office. I said "no, I don't want to run for office". Miss Intellect qualified and we left laughing at what had happened. On the way home, Miss Intellect called personally our friends Helaine, the chairman of Orchard County, and others and they could not believe who I was; the first Just Say No Kid. When we left Saturday morning for the Orchard County Republican Party, we got there and everyone treated us differently, although some honchos of the District Attorney Livingstone were still treating us badly or ignoring us. The others treated us like heroes and let us know that we were always welcome to the party. We had two federal agents come talk to us. They had just returned from California and they let us know that Nancy Reagan sent her best regards. One agent went outside to mom, she was smoking, and he informed her that they did believe I was innocent and was hung. Mom told them that we were going to continue to fight the felony charge. The agent said "good luck, I hope you can". I walked out with the other agent and told the one talking to mom "we have all the evidence and proof to back us up". We moved, once again by court order, to a little house. The landlord was a serious pervert. He didn't want me and mom to move in because he kept eying my sister and wanted her to move in instead. Every time we left, we would lock the doors, but every time we got back they would be unlocked or wide open, or both. We kept having problems with the landlord fixing things and his niece, who lived next door, called me to the fence one day and said she was going to get an animal trap, but the trap was not for our pets. I asked her not to with a tape recorder in my hand recording the conversation. She got the trap anyway and I got a harness for our cat to walk him on a leash. I was at one of the carwashes and the Chief Magistrate was there washing his car. I got to talking to him about this woman getting an animal trap and showed him a flier I had made about it. He said "Wunderlich, I will look into it and ill have the trap picked up this afternoon, or ill have it where she will keep it in the front yard with a sign that has the number for animal control. On Fridays at three pm the trap must be closed until Monday unless it's a weekend, then it will be allowed to be open on Tuesday". The landlord's niece decided it wasn't worth her time to cater to the trap so she had the trap picked up under the judge's orders. She also tried to have a warrant put out for me for the flier but her request was denied. The landlord showed up and he started taking up the flags that were around our yard saying "you can't have any signs of any kind in my yard". I said "these aren't signs, they're flags". He said "I don't want any signs, flags, anything here on my property. I have a warrant out for your arrest". I went inside the house and called the law. I asked them to send an officer because there may be a warrant out for my arrest. The law came and asked him if there was indeed a warrant out for my arrest and the landlord said "no, I was trying to scare him". The officer told the landlord "trying to intimidate someone with a phony warrant is against the law". The landlord told the officer "I guess the reason you're taking his side is because he's been asked to run for mayor". The officer said "That has nothing to do with it". The officer then turned to me and said "do you intend on running for mayor". The landlord told the officer that he didn't want us living there any longer and the landlord was instructed by the officer that he had to go downtown to file paperwork if he wanted us to vacate. The landlord filed the paperwork for eviction under the grounds of us having unauthorized pets on the property. Before we had the hearing for the eviction, on September 1st 2005, I was called to the probation office and the state restored 110% of my rights. We left the probation office and went straight to the Board of Elections with a card from the state and I got the reregistered to vote. We went to the eviction hearing and the bailiff instructed us on court proceeding. Throughout the hearing, the landlord showed no respect for the court and didn't conduct himself according to what the bailiff had said. The judge asked us if we had permission to have the pets and we said yes, and we let him listen to a tape of the landlord coming to fix the sink and our dog was growling and barking at him. The judge turned to our landlord and said "well it seems like the dog is there and he has no use for you so feel inclined that you did in fact give them permission to have their pets". The landlord showed further disrespect saying "no, I did not give them anything in *writing* stating that I gave them permission for their pets". The judge said "well, their front door was always open, that's stated in their initial statement". The landlord said "I have the right to go in there and check my property". The judge said "no, not when you rent out the property to someone else... my verdict is that the next two months will be rent free for Mr. Wunderlich and you will not got back onto the property until it comes time to inspect the property with the tenants, and as long as there is no damages to the property, you will give back their deposit".

On the day we moved, we contacted the landlord several times trying to get him to come and inspect it before we left. We also had paid the last two months rent so that we would have the bank statements in order to buy our next house. We ended up having to go back to the court to get our deposit back because he wouldn't give us our deposit back. While signing the papers for our new house, the real estate agent representing the property owners stole all the window curtains and mini blinds. I checked the trash to see if they had been thrown away; nothing was in it. Before moving into the new house, all the wiring had to be redone so we could turn the power on. We called our electric company and they rewired the box and put new braces on the supply line wire. The total cost was $314. The company also replaced the power outlets because they were burned out.

We started moving into our home and it was a very blissful time in our lives. We met one of our neighbors, Miss Anna; she was a very sweet lady. Anna always came over and spoke to me. After, we met another woman who was very spiteful and mean to me; Ms. Loveless.

Before we actually moved in, federal agents came to the house and took pictures and measured the driveways. When Ms. Loveless saw the agents doing this, they told her that I was under federal protection but they wouldn't say why. Ms. Loveless started telling all the neighbors that we were bad people and criminals. She even had her son, grandson, and other family members, come to her house and blow all the leaves that fell off her trees into our yard. I tried talking to her but that didn't work. I called for a county Marshall and he caught them doing it. He was going to cite her but I told him not to because her age, health, and the fact that I wanted to live in peace with her in the neighborhood.

Miss Anna told her that we were good people and it finally sank in. Unfortunately, Ms. Loveless passed away before she could apologize, but her family came by and apologized to us.

Anna's power lines went through the woods, so she lost power often. We always helped her because she was a great friend and we believe in helping people. We had a rainstorm and we supplied her with ice, cooked meals, and shared with her. Miss Anna had lost power during an ice storm and almost froze to death. Mom and I were leaving the house around 11:30 am and she came over and stopped us. She had no power, phone, or cable. I called the power company and they said the soonest the power could be restored is 6:30 pm. I told them that that wouldn't do and they told me there was nothing I could do. I told them "bet me". I hung up the phone and called the Mayor and City Commissions on their personal lines (I would've called their offices but this was on a Saturday). By the time I got off the phone to check on mom, a woman from the power company drove up and said "I'm here now, no more calls are needed". This made me laugh. The power was restored in an hour. After the neighbors saw us helping Anna so much, they started coming over and invited us to their churches and meetings. We had been accepted as good neighbors. We had new neighbors move into Ms. Loveless's house who turned out to be good neighbors. Scott and were good Christian people and every time they saw me outside they would wave and come over and talk. Scott even offered to fix any car trouble if we had any. We also got another new neighbor a couple months after named Mr. Wilson.

Mr. Wilson is a Vietnam war veteran and a very good man. He knows how to fix and repair homes and sheds, and he loved my mom's home cooking. We would sometimes share dinner with him and he would share his garden with us. Mom specialty is fried green tomatoes and he would always bring her green tomatoes for her to cook. We felt blessed, having three amazing neighbors. Unfortunately, Miss Anna had to move because her tightwad landlord refused to fix her gas and hot water heater. I helped her move and occasionally helped her when she needed help or groceries. Just before she moved, she went into the hospital and I would bring her mail and magazines to her room. After she got out of the hospital, she got a new apartment that had security. It was a very nice place and she was very lucky to have found it considering her income and the fact she was living alone. Nobody has moved into her old home, and it sits vacant to this day.

In 2006, I charged the District Attorney Livingstone under Articles of Impeachment and he was legally served. The District Attorney Livingstone never answered to my charges. In fact, he actually got one of his friends, the Clerk of the Court, to send me a full refund for the filing fee and the serving fee. That same year, October 13, 2006, we bought our own house and no pompous judge or District Attorney Livingstone could force us out of our home anymore. We decided to wait and see what happens. Superior Court Judge and Chief Judge retired and both went into senior status before I got off probation. Chief went on to be sheriff. Our friend Congressman Charles died in 2007.

We took Ms. Intellect, after her family neglected her, under our wing and let her move into our house after the state had put her into a personal care home and they wouldn't feed them hardly anything. When she started complaining about not being fed enough, I visited her one day, and I was given the choice of either taking her or giving her back to her family to be further abused and neglected. We took her in and I called around to try and get her some furniture so she could sleep comfortably. I ended up calling our friend State Representative Angela, who was in the hospital on account of her husband. She said that she would have to return my call and about 40 minutes later she called me back. She informed me to start looking for a bed but not a used one. I went looking for a bed, and I found one at Five Star Bedding and when I mentioned Representative Angela and how she was going to pay for it, he said "oh sure". We got the bed and we called other mutual friends to help with her medications.

The people started listening to us more about the District Attorney Livingstone's daughter killed a girl in her car when she was in a car accident. They didn't test her for DUI. She ran a stop sign and they kept trying to charge the other driver. Finally, no charges were filed on this case, as far as I know. The District

Attorney Livingstone said that his daughter is in a coma and that's punishment enough. God knows that if it had been anyone else then they would've been charged. Soon after, the District Attorney Livingstone sent friends and family to the Governor. He appointed moms choice for judgeship, Heat. He promised never to appoint the District Attorney Livingstone but then lied. He appointed the District Attorney Livingstone judgeship. At first we were very angry at his lie. Later, the former governor sent us a message that for our own safety he appointed the District Attorney Livingstone his judgeship to lessen his power. We had lost our friend Congressman Charles; he was a longtime friend and he worked with the Secretary of State Mary Green to restore my rights before his death. The newly appointed Sheriff apologized to me for taking sides in the ordeal that cost me five years of my life and caused moms health to get worse at times. Thank God mom has better days than worse one. Sheriff told me that he tells his officers to show us respect when we call and the bottom line; leave us alone. Some officers didn't listen to him and they kept trying to challenge us. We defeated them before court or the prosecutor moved to dismiss the case before it went before the judge. The officers either resigned or were fired. In 2008 the Orchard County Republican Party and state party paid the District Attorney Livingstone $500.00 to come join their party against our wishes and we told them this would be a huge mistake. We didn't tell anyone of the fully enforce war plans from our friend General Four Star. We started putting the plan in place with no one knowing what we were doing. We had to wait for Sheriff to get out of office. The man that he gave the felony charge to was caught shooting a man twice and punching him and he even raped a woman inside his home. Our former neighbor was arrested and then other states found out and they wanted him. One charge was for gang-raping a 13 year old girl and the other in a different state was for him raping a 14 year old girl. Sheriff, after our former neighbor's first arrest on Friday, called a press conference to announce his retirement on the following Monday. We decided then to fully emplace the war plan. We started putting up the signs in our front yard and we started going to meetings again. This time we were very vocal in confronting the corruption head-on. The Citizens for Good Government voted to have us banned from their good old' boy meetings full of politicians that don't want to hear what they were doing wrong. We started educating the citizens about the corruption and they started treating us with respect. They even started asking me to run for mayor, Congress, and even Governor. I always replied with "no, no thank you". We started working on getting the warrants system and jury selections changed. Now, a warrant must be applied for and a hearing has to take place with evidence proving a crime. The jury clerks are no longer appointed by the Chief Judge and the juries are no longer hand-picked by the court. The State Supreme Court, after hearing our complaints and the complaints of others, started doing jury selection in Orchard County by lottery.

One day I was at Major Superstore and the District Attorney Livingstone looked over the produce display at me and said "hi buddy", not recognizing me from all the weight I had lost. I looked him in the eye and said "I am NOT your Damn Buddy; I am the one who will destroy you". He started walking away and I said "hey! We know where your child rapist witness is and we will tell everyone how you won your cases as District Attorney Livingstone". He got really embarrassed when people were standing around him and listening to me telling him what kind of a man he was. I told him "you knew I was innocent and you still wanted me after charging you with assault and I have an order for a warrant to be signed once you are no longer in office, don't I". He ran out of Major Superstore red-faced. Mom and I were going into Kroger the following week and the District Attorney Livingstone was leaving and mom saw him first and said "Hi Mr. Impeached". He started running away, red-faced again.

I had a legal matter I had to take care of that had nothing to do with my case or ordeal. We went before Assistant Magistrate and he asked the other party "do you know Mr. Wunderlich". They said no. Assistant Magistrate said "let me educate you on Mr. Wunderlich, he is a very good and honest young man. I have known him and his mother for years. They ALWAYS come to court ready to win the case and with evidence. They know the law, and wait a minute, Mr. Wunderlich..". I said "yes, Your Honor". He asked "do you still have the power of pro-se Mr. Wunderlich". I said "yes, Your Honor". He then looked at the other party and said "do you really want to pursue this matter, because I can tell you that Mr. Wunderlich is ready to use his protections given to him by the law". He then asked me "is this correct Mr. Wunderlich". I answered "yes, Your Honor". Assistant Magistrate said "are you still on probation". I said "Jesus Christ Judge, how long does you and corrupt the District Attorney Livingstone think I would be punished for, it ended 2005". Assistant Magistrate said "okay, Mr. Wunderlich, what have you been doing now". I said "I am writing a book on the corruption in our judicial system, and the law of our town. The District Attorney Livingstone and friends are the stars in my book ". I also informed the courtroom that my family is watching what's happening with me and my mom. Assistant Magistrate said "who is your family Mr. Wunderlich". I said "read the book of Gangsters of California by the Author. It mentions my father, uncles, aunts, and cousins by name". Assistant Magistrate said "that makes you the baby of the gangsters and mobsters"? I said "yes, and First Lady Nancy Reagan has just confirmed me as being the first Just Say No Kid, I gave her the slogan in 1976. If the District Attorney Livingstone or anyone else tries to do anything more than we are very much ready to answer then with pin-point accuracy by facts on paper and by 'other means'". Assistant Magistrate said "what is your plan then". I said "Judge, we are following the war plan of one of our friend Gen. Four Star. He told us we couldn't stop the District Attorney Livingstone and the others by hurting us with their powers, but he told my mother and I how to destroy their power using free speech and posting signs in our front yard". Assistant Magistrate said "Okay Mr. Wunderlich", he turned to the prosecutor and said "do you wish to dismiss your claim against Mr. Wunderlich if he dismisses his case against you"? Both the prosecutor and I agreed to do that. Assistant Magistrate said "Mr. Wunderlich, please tell your mother I send my best regards". I reminded Assistant Magistrate of the warrant order we had from him for the District Attorney Livingstone. He said, rubbing his head, "Oh my God Mr. Wunderlich, well, if you claim this then I guess I must've ordered it". As I was getting ready to leave Assistant Magistrate said "I wish to have my bailiff escort you to your truck to make sure that no harm come to you leaving the courthouse". I said "Judge, that isn't necessary". He said "I would feel safer having you escorted, knowing who your family is". I finally agreed and said "okay, thank you". As I was leaving I turned to him and said "Tell the District Attorney Livingstone that I said hello". I knew he was in his chambers listening to the hearing. Assistant Magistrate said "I think he probably heard you already". I said "I know he is somewhere in this new courthouse and I want him to know that I am ready for whatever he wants to do, The District Attorney Livingstone said in a meeting at the Pride in Progress that when you wrong someone, you must pay compensation or restitution". Assistant Magistrate asked me "How much are you trying to get"? I said "one million dollars, his friends and family can sell hot dogs to save his buns and the buns of this county and state". Assistant Magistrate said "I will inform the District Attorney Livingstone of the amount you are seeking". I said "thank you, there's no room for compromising or making a deal, the District Attorney Livingstone has nothing to bargain with; he has lost". I exited the courtroom, walking tall and upright, proud to know I gave my message to the county and state. I got to my truck and called mom and told her that we had won another case, I also told her the details of what happened in the courtroom. She said "that's great Wunderlich, hurry home and change clothes and let's talk about our next move".

We started writing the book and the District Attorney Livingstone had me confronted at the gym around 9 pm by a friend of his. His friend wanted his "ten seconds of fame" and he called the law on me accusing me of being a gangster. When the officer arrived, we went into a meeting room in the gym. I used my federal power and told the officer to sit down and he resisted so I said "you either sit down or I leave right now; the only thing that will stop me is if you charge me, or shoot me". The officer said "I will sit down". After he sat, I said "yes, I am the baby of gangsters and mobsters and what this county and state has done to me is very wrong. Using their powers to get over on honest citizens makes them a bunch of common criminals in my eyes. Ronald Reagan must have been right when he said 'when you have absolute power, you have absolute corruption absolutely'. He must have met Chief Judge and the others when coming to the state". I started to leave and the officer said "I'm not going to file any reports about coming to this gym tonight, this is the end of it". The next afternoon, a man came to the house, and knocked on the door. Mom asked "who is it". The man answered "police". Mom looked at me and we both thought 'we don't have any police in Orchard County'. Mom answered the door with her gun drawn and she said "are you some more of the corrupt sheriff's department". The agent that answered the door said "we aren't from the sheriff's department, I'm Agent Carmel from the F.B.I.". The agents both flashed their badges in the glass, the badges clearly saying Federal Bureau of Investigations. They stood on the porch and insisted only that my mother address the District Attorney Livingstone as "Judge". She said "Judge my ASS, he hasn't earned the title". The agent asked my mom to put the gun away and she said "no, but I will put the safety on". The agent said that he wanted to talk to me. My mom said "all you better do is talk, on second thought, go ahead and arrest him because that will be one way to put an end to all their corruption once and for all. Our family is watching and helping us". The agent wrote on a piece of paper:

Investigator Carmel   F.B.I. Task Force 7##-2##-6###

Mom told him, "I am a former officer". Mom overheard them shaking their heads and saying "wow, that's one tough lady". Mom was very excited when she called me. I called Investigator Carmel back using the phone number on the paper and he said "Wunderlich, come to my office at the F.B.I. headquarters for the area". I went and waited for them to get there, assuming they were across town with their buddy the District Attorney Livingstone across town telling him what my mother had said. When they finally showed up, one of the agents tried to search me and I looked at Carmel and asked "Am I under arrest". He said "no, not at this time". I said "then you cannot search me, Hell, I wouldn't hurt my government or you, I was told to come to this office and the door was locked". I was in there with three F.B.I. agents. They said that they wanted to read my book, and I knew this was a violation of my privacy rights, but with the three agents in one office with me alone, I was afraid of what would happen if I refused them. When I called the District Attorney Livingstone corrupt, they quickly said "You WILL refer to him as Judge". I said "No, I will never call that man judge". I showed them the pictures and one was a mug shot of Jack. It made me laugh, one of the agents said "That looks like a mug shot". I said "very good, you know a mug shot when you see one". I knew that this was just a ploy to get details about the book because they were only interested in these details and they gave me no Miranda warning or even told me why I was told to be there. Investigator Carmel continued to lie when he said "we will try to get you justice and correct the injustice that was done to you and your mother. How much money do you want for restitution and compensation"? I said "One million Dollars". Mr. Carmel said "that's not enough". I said "I want justice and what's fair". The interview felt more like an interrogation. I told them "they cost us 2 homes, 1 work shed, $80,000 in debt, we had to sell everything we owned to' fight this 5 plus years probation fees and fines". I looked at Carmel "I hope you are federal". He asked "why would you ask that". I said "I have federal powers of pro-se and was accused of not knowing what my powers are, but I just choose to use them and not abuse them. I have a court order for a warrant for the District Attorney Livingstone and the order will be executed when he is no longer in power". After the meeting, Mr. Carmel said "this is a 'death book'". I looked at him and said "yes, I know what they are capable of doing, and evidently, you know it too". I left them and called my mother and let her know I was okay. Mom said "hurry home so we can work on the war plans". I told her that Mr. Carmel had asked me to not publish the book until he had investigated it. We delayed it for 30 days, as if this was a joke or a delaying tactic. We decided to write this book, and include this meeting. Investigator Carmel highly encouraged me and even said that I WILL NOT include this meeting in the book. After a while, I learned, after the help they had promised us, they lied and they weren't going to help us at all.

The District Attorney Livingstone must've wanted to get rid of Carmel because they knew we had a camera up and we recorded everything. My feeling is that the District Attorney Livingstone wanted to intimidate me by using Carmel and the two other phony agents. I think that maybe Mr. Carmel had knew too much about him and the others in power. About a week after the agents came, I was sitting in a fast food restaurant skyping a friend of mine, and what do you know, the District Attorney Livingstone walks in. He overheard me and thought I was talking to him and he said "are you talking to me". I looked at him and said "no, I wouldn't talk to you if you were the only one here. You are a liar, you are corrupt, and you are under investigation for what you've done to me, my mother, and others". The District Attorney Livingstone was also caught giving a thieving coroner debit cards, credit cards, cars, jewelry, and other property of people that had passed away. The coroner is in jail now awaiting prosecution and the District Attorney Livingstone is under investigation for that also. The District Attorney Livingstone looked at me and said "Wunderlich, you are under investigation also". I laughed and said "what, from your houseboy and puppy dog Carmel, you must be kidding or are you trying to get rid of him". He walked away and a man in the restaurant stopped him and said "oh, you are the Judge". He stood proud. I felt like the guy was put there just to boost the District Attorney Livingstone, I laughed. The man said "you ARE the Honorable Judge". I started cracking up bad. He said "Yes I am". I snorted "yes he is and he's a liar and corrupt, he is a common criminal. Tell him of the articles of impeachment I filed against you, the charges you been running away from answering every since. I'm not afraid of you, I have all the proof of your lies and the corruption and you really should read the book Famous Gangsters of California by the Author so you know who my family is, and who you are challenging. Just before my father passed, he told me I would bring the family together. Guess what, the family is together, and thanks to you and your family and friends, my father's prophecy has come true. You are anything but honorable". He turned red faced and stormed out of the restaurant.

We stopped going to the Republican functions because they started mistreating us due to our vocality of the District Attorney Livingstone. We started voting American style, and stopped caring about the 'R' or the 'D' next to the candidates' names. Let the best one win. Unfortunately though, in the state I live in, we have no bipartisanship in the running, so we have party and racial divides.

The courts for the State couldn't care less for an honest citizen being hung for crime that wasn't committed, and they use lies and hearsay to win cases at any cost. They would go as far as using county and state employees on juries. And these employees would always push for a guilty verdict to save their families and their jobs. Our Founding Fathers would be rolling over in their graves if they knew how the State discards the U.S. Constitution and the Law. We had citizens come and tell us we were pissing in the wind because there was no winning against our government. This made us even more determined to get the truth out. We were still mistreated by corrupt friends and family of the District Attorney Livingstone, but that didn't matter; we kept fighting anyway.

In May of 2014, we read in the newspapers that Mr. Carmel was only an investigator for the sheriff's department and that he had indeed committed a felony impersonation an F.B.I. agent in the F.B.I. Task Force. I called the Sheriff and his office was under some order not to connect any citizen's calls to him personally. I was connected with one Lieutenant Stubby and he was very rude to me, and he even threatened me with jail if I came down to the office to file any complaint against Carmel. I sent a letter to Sheriff, newly appointed District Attorney Livingstone, the new Governor, US Attorney General, and F.B.I. Headquarters in Washington D.C., telling them of this instance and of Carmel. Nothing was done of course.

I ran into Lieutenant Stubby at Sam's Club and I asked him what he was going to charge me with for sending the letter. He said that he was going to charge me with causing a problem with the sheriff's department and causing problems for Investigator Carmel. He also informed me that Carmel had been given a volunteer F.B.I. badge to use only for F.B.I. business, but Carmel, being a power-abuser, tried to use the badge to intimidate us. I am very disappointed with how Sheriff Dingo handled this situation and how the other agencies ignored the fact that Carmel had abused the power of his badge.

I went to see my sister Cowgirl this past June and the trip was amazing. I made it to Kansas from here in two days! Even though I was caught in a rainstorm along the way. When I got there, Sister Cowgirl wanted to travel back with me but it wasn't allowed; she wanted me to sneak her out of the nursing home. I told her I would be back the next morning, and when I got there I told her that I would take her with me but I couldn't because she couldn't walk to my truck and they would probably have me arrested for endangerment and kidnapping. Sister Cowgirl said she didn't want me to go to jail and I told her I didn't want to go to jail either. When I was leaving, I was so tired of paying the tolls that when I stopped at a toll booth I told the operator "goodbye forever, I will never pay a toll again where I'm going and if the state ever gets tolls, I will personally kick them out of office. I called mom and she said "come on home". I said "I love you mom". She said "I love you too Wunderlich, drive carefully". I said "I will, I'll see you soon, I love you too". On the way home, I drove through Tornado Alley, they had dozens of tornado warnings and I started to drive faster going through those states. On the way, I saw Teddy Roosevelts Air Force One Plane and I was so honored to be so close to it. I passed by a casino that was along the way, it offered $50 just to stop in and so I did. I went in and they gave me $50 to use however I wanted. I took my 50 and went to the casinos buffet and had a steak dinner that cost about $21. I ate and started to leave. I passed by a nice old woman that was having bad luck at her slot machine. I went over and gave her the rest of the money and said "may God bless you, good luck". As I was exiting the front doors, a man came to me and said "thank you for coming". I said "Thanks, the buffet was awesome", and I left. I was back on the road again and all was good until the freeway I was on turned into one lane, and the high traffic became bumper to bumper. I was happy to see that the freeway went two-laned again and I had to detour so I exited. I got lost once I got off and kept driving on the roads trying to get back to the freeway.

I found an on-ramp, but a sign was posted "permanent residence or trucks only, all others will be ticketed". I was about to use it but saw an officer drive up behind me. I turned into a gas station instead and he followed and stopped next to me. "You must be lost", the officer said. I said yes. He said "well why don't you just follow me and I'll get you back up onto the freeway in the right direction". I said thank you and followed him back onto the freeway. I was on my way again but a bad storm started coming in and the fog was too thick to drive in. I called mom and she said to stop and get a room, which would make my drive back three days now. I stopped at a motel that had a picture framed of a famous fisherman on the wall of the lobby. The sign on the front desk said it was $99 a night but since I knew the man that was working that night, I got a room for $59. I got to my room and noticed that the bed was taller than my waist! I went to the front desk and asked for a lower bed because for some reason, when I'm at hotels and motels, I fall out of the bed. They told me that this was the only room that they had so I said okay. I went back to my room and the phone was ringing. It was my friend, a pro-fisherman, and we sat and talked for a while about fishing and other things. I got finished talking to him and called mom to tell her that I had got a room. I then ordered some pizza and ate and went to sleep.

The next morning, I was back on my way again. I called mom when traffic was stopped due to 7 or 8 deer running across the street. I arrived home and mom gave me a hug and a kiss and said "thank God you're home". We started thinking about what to do for dinner. We ordered Hibachi take-out.

We talked about what the family had told me about Jack and his brother-in-law legal troubles and they said "we are ready to help you kid, and the sweetheart of the family". A week later, I was sitting at McDonalds and an old man came and sat down and called me MASTER. I said "who are you and how are we related". He said he was my cousin and also said what the family calls him, and then, he asked me for a dollar. I looked at him crazily "what do you need a dollar for". He said that one dollar would get rid of all the troublemakers. I told my cousin "I don't believe in violence, I'm writing a book and that's how I will get justice and make millions". I called mom after our conversation and she said "Holy Shit, what is he doing there". After I told her of our conversation, she said to give him the dollar and write on it "the only way anything should be done is if something happens to us, then you can take care of business".

On July 29th I celebrated my birthday and mom bought me a computer, printer, and Hibachi take-out. We put up more signs in our yard and we sent letters to newly elected Sheriff Dingo, newly elected District Attorney Ms. Snow, newly elected Governor and to the U.S. Attorney General letting them know of the criminal actions of the investigator Carmel.

This past October, the officers in the Sheriff's Department were caught using steroids and other drugs. The Sheriff won't test them, or charge them.

All is okay for now. We have finished writing the book, the one you are finished reading, and thank God I'm still alive. I was fearful due to the corruption by the newly elected District Attorney Ms. Snowy, Chief Judge and Superior Court Judge, Former Sheriff, Newly Elected Sheriff, the Clerk of the Court, and Jack and his brother-in-law. I thought I would've been killed by what they have done or they would do it themselves.

Now that this is out, I'm no longer afraid. Be aware, this could happen to you. Watch your government, wherever you are, and take your stand against corruption and mistreatment.

9 781955 070171